A LONG TIME COMING

A Lyrical Biography of Race in America from Ona Judge to Barack Obama

Ray Anthony Shepard   Art by R. Gregory Christie

CALKINS CREEK
AN IMPRINT OF ASTRA BOOKS FOR YOUNG READERS
New York

This is a work of creative nonfiction told in five story-poems—flash lines of verse, prose, and quotes—anchored in historical facts. Nonfiction in verse may sound like an oxymoron, a mash-up gone astray, as awful as a sardines-and-sauerkraut breakfast sandwich. Instead, I hope to serve you banana and peanut butter spread on a toasted sesame seed bagel—delicious, but not your usual fare. Nonfiction in verse is my way to tell a story of race in the lives of six American historymakers who helped *form a more perfect Union*: Ona Judge, Frederick Douglass, Harriet Tubman, Ida B. Wells, Martin Luther King Jr., and Barack Obama.

I have not attempted to tell their complete life stories. Instead, I present scenes from significant events that show how they tilted the country's moral arc toward liberty, freedom, and justice to make the United States the world's first major multiethnic democracy. These scenes are authentic moments inspired by real and confirmed facts of our country's heroic and continuing struggle to become an inclusive democracy. In place of quotation marks, I have *italicized all quotes* and listed their references in the sources notes. Also, I have capitalized *Black* and *White* when pertaining to race.

—*Ray Anthony Shepard*
Lincoln, Massachusetts

A NOTE TO THE READER

These story-poems are poetic profiles of resilient lives, revealing the natural and universal desire for fairness. These fact-based profiles are tied together like chapters in a novel. It is my way of showing the legacy of race in American history and our lives. —RAS

CONTENTS

DID YOU EVER WONDER? 9

PART I: 1773-1913
   ENSLAVEMENT AND EMANCIPATION 10-117
      Ona Judge
      Frederick Douglass and Harriet Tubman

PART II: 1862-1968
   FREEDOM AND JUSTICE 118-251
      Ida B. Wells
      Martin Luther King Jr.

PART III: 1961-2008
   THE PROMISE OF AMERICA 252-297
      Barack Obama

   EPILOGUE 299
   THE LONG STRUGGLE 303
      Timeline
   HISTORY CLIPS 313
   FURTHER READING 313
   ACKNOWLEDGMENTS 315
   BIBLIOGRAPHY AND SOURCE NOTES 316
   INDEX 324
   ABOUT THE AUTHOR 331

For Mom and Dad,
who—in the thunder and lightning—
taught their eleven to ride
the wings of the storm
—*RAS*

Dedicated to Lonnie Myer
—*RGC*

Children have never been very good at listening to their elders,
but they have never failed to imitate them.

—James Baldwin

DID YOU EVER WONDER?

Why there were the unfreed
in the land of the free?

Why seven hundred and fifty thousand
soldiers—White, Black, Union,
Confederate—died to keep
or free the unfreed?

Why a decade later the freed
were once again unfreed?

Why a century later
civil rights civilians—
Black, White, southerners,
northerners—died
freeing the unfreed once again?

Or wonder why
we separate, perpetuate, and
hyphenate some Americans
as if the hyphen means
more or less American?

PERSONAL HISTORY

As a fifth-grader at Bancroft School,
I cringed during slavery's history time
as one of the few Black faces
on Nebraska's Great White Plains.
The class, unable to see
we were chained together
in American history,
turned to me to explain
what their great-great-grandparents
did to mine.

PART I

1773-1913

Enslavement and Emancipation

ONA JUDGE
c. 1773-1848

The Woman
Who Stole Herself

*I am free now,
and choose to remain so.*

—Ona Judge

ONA JUDGE

Not long ago lived a *nearly white* girl
who had no shoes and two tattered smocks
spun of rough cotton, one for summer
and one for winter.

Her mistress and master—
Martha and George Washington—
called her Oney.
She called herself Ona
the name her mama gave her.

No matter her name
on a dreaded day, Ona
was summoned to the mansion house
to learn how she would spend
the rest of her days enslaved.

The mistress of Mount Vernon
did not trouble about which year
or day a slave was born
yet knew when Black and nearly White
girls and boys had ripened beyond
chores for little arms and legs:
>no more picking herbs
>in the kitchen garden,
>no more toting
>smelly chamber pots.

Martha Washington knew
it was time for Ona
to do the grown-up work
of slavery's endless days.

SEPARATION DAY

Ona, thought to be ten
rubbed her dirty toes
on the carpeted floor
in one of the many mansion rooms
painted blue, green, or yellow.
Ona's Separation Day:
Would the mistress proclaim her a scullery maid
to scrape and scrub pots and pans
in the smoky kitchen, or a laundry maid
to bend over vats in that steaming room
or declare Ona a field hand
planting and picking wheat and rye,
work that would spend and bend Ona
in a few short years?

> Or would the color of her skin
> paler than her mama's—"Mulatto" Betty—
> make her a privileged slave?

THE FAIRY QUEEN

The mistress wore a gown
fluffed with wings
as if a fairy queen.
She waved her hand
and soft linen dresses appeared
for Ona's *slender* frame,
leather shoes for her tiny feet,
and a white cap for her *bushy black hair.*
She would learn her mother's art
sewing Virginia cloth
into victory gowns to celebrate
General Washington
who'd sent King George's red-coated
soldiers back across the sea
and made America free.

This was the best job a slave could have.
Betty was mama proud.
Her daughter would have a softer life.
Ona thanked her Mount Vernon mistress
but in a secret spot of her being
she knew having the best job
a slave could have
was not nearly enough.

ONA'S MAMA

Before Mount Vernon, before Ona,
Martha Custis was a widow and wealthy
at twenty-six, inheritor of acres of land
and the services of many slaves
including Ona's mother Betty.
When George Washington
tall, handsome, soldier, surveyor,
courted and married Martha,
she selected and herded
eighty-four chosen slaves to Mount Vernon,
among them Betty and her
baby son, Austin.
Betty was called a mulatto
to signal her father was White,
a man who did not claim her,
which might explain
why she had no last name.

ONA'S DADDY

A down-and-out Englishman,
Andrew Judge indentured himself
for a better life in America.
He tailored George Washington's broadcloth suits
and when his servant time was up,
he stayed to be with Betty, Ona,
and her new baby sister, Delphy,
all enslaved, and could not leave
Mount Vernon.
A free White man living across
the color line required more courage
than Andrew Judge could long maintain.
In 1781 he took his leave
free as Ona could never be.
Ona must have wondered
why her daddy's whiteness set him free
while her mother's darker shade locked
her and the children in slavery's cage.
Betty had to explain: Virginia law ruled
the child of a woman enslaved
was but a baby slave.
It didn't matter that her daddy
was English and White.
Betty also had to tell
her freedom-dreaming daughter:
Being Martha Washington's
special slave and personal maid

would protect her from certain men's desire
to have complete control
of a slave woman's body and soul.

HER MAMA'S WARNING

The Washingtons did not allow slaves
to read or write or record the days
so we do not know when Betty told the story
that must have made Ona shiver:
Back in 1766, George Washington
caught Negro Tom escaping,
had him whipped and locked in a room
neither blue, yellow, nor green
but dark as a tomb, before he sold
the *Rogue & Runaway*
for a few bottles of rum
and sent poor Tom to waste away
cutting sugar cane under the searing sun
and a Barbados whip.

Mount Vernon
1783–1789

MISTRESS OF THE NEEDLE

Ona spent the next six years
pleasing her mistress
who was just as pleased
she had granted Ona Judge

the best job a slave could have.
Ona stitched and sewed
and became *a mistress of her needle*
though she could not stop
her warring thoughts
for and against freedom-running.

The fate of Negro Tom
she'd not forgotten
but another fear held Ona in place:
the President's toothache.
A fifty-year-old dental problem
kept him in a perpetual frown.
A long-ago boyish show of manly strength
cracking walnuts between his pearlies
had made his mouth
a menagerie of broken pieces.
Behind his frightening scowl
danced a bridge of hippopotamus bone
a horse tooth too tall
a donkey tooth too short and
    nine teeth from certain nameless Negroes
    thirteen shillings apiece.

FIRST MAID

When Ona was thought to be sixteen
America elected George Washington
President and sent him to New York City
to sit atop the new government.

Ona's master was America's first President
and her mistress the country's first Grand Lady.
Ona's brother Austin was First Waiter
at the President's dining table.
Ona Judge, America's First Maid.

Ona belonged to the country's
most powerful family.
She traveled with her mistress
to fancy parlor parties hosted
by the finest and wealthiest.
She glowed in the warmth of praise
for her care of America's Grand Lady.

Philadelphia
November 1790

LIBERTY BELL

The government moved to Philadelphia
and the Washingtons, Ona,
and eight others enslaved
moved into the President's House on High Street.
From there, Ona could hear the State House bell.
Twice-cracked, it rang to call some men
to vote.
Or it rang when there was something to report.
The bell had rung for liberty—
for the Declaration of Independence
in which all were not yet equal,
for the signing of the Constitution,
which was not yet fair.
It's doubtful seventeen-year-old Ona,
a member of America's most famous family,
weighed these heavy concerns.
But on occasion, doubts sneaked
into her thoughts.

DOUBTS

City streets teemed with Blacks,
some enslaved, some free.
One group came and went as they pleased.
The other lived at their masters' beck and call.
Thoughts of escape appealed.

Yet Ona had a wardrobe of fancy clothes,
a dollar now and then to spend.
She did not have to hawk fruit
in the market square,
pick through garbage
for rags to sell or food to eat.
She did not have to sleep
on cobblestone streets.

When Eliza, Martha's eldest grandchild,
came for a visit, she and Ona
went among flirting men
who greeted the young ladies
from the rich and famous family.
On these occasions, Ona doubted
Negro Tom's fate, forgot
George Washington's frown.
When freedom pulled at her
she cast it away with questions:

      Where would she go?
      How would she live?
      Who would show her the way?
      Who would take her in?

ANSWERS

As Ona went about the city
Free Blacks whispered:
If she wanted to run
they would show her the way.
Members of the African Methodist Episcopal Church

said they would take her in.
Ona closed her ears, out of fear,
clinging to the life she knew.
She lived in the President's House,
was part of the Washington family—
or so she thought.
Granddaughter Eliza was making
her feel otherwise, with boss
and sass, demands and nasty grumbles.
Eliza showed Ona who was family
and who was not.

Philadelphia

A VELVET CAGE

After a day of traveling from tea to tea
making certain no hair was out of place
no spot was on her mistress's dress,
Ona helped the Grand Lady slip from her
complicated clothes into a simple nightgown
ready for bed.
Ona no longer thought
Martha Washington grand
when she saw blemishes and pockmarks
of age.
After a day of dressing and caring
for the Lady, Ona returned to her room
to stitch and mend before she could sleep.
Outside this room, her velvet cage,
she could hear freedom ring,

the twice-cracked State House bell
had rung for liberty but not for her.

Philadelphia
1793

FUGITIVES

Too many of America's enslaved
wanted to breathe freedom's air,
ran north for a fresher breeze.

Too many slaveowners became alarmed,
demanded all windows be shut.

Congress agreed, as did the President
who had lost a slave or two
during the Revolutionary War.
He signed the Fugitive Slave Act,
made runaway slaves outlaws!

If Ona escaped, the Washingtons
had a stronger law to grab her back.

DECEIVED

Ona, thought to be twenty-one,
was surprised by the President's generosity.
He sent her to Mount Vernon twice a year
to see her mother Betty who was further
bent and spent by slavery's endless days.
Free Blacks pulled her aside,
whispered, don't be fooled.
Pennsylvania law set a slave free
if they were twenty-one and kept
in the state six consecutive months.
George Washington sent her back
to restart her slavery clock.

Havre de Grace, Maryland
December 1794

AUSTIN

A blow harder than deceit hit Ona's heart.
Brother Austin, on his way to Mount Vernon
to restart his slavery's clock
fell from his horse
crossing a Maryland stream,
cracked his head.
Dead at thirty-seven.

Mount Vernon
January 1795

BETTY

Another death for Ona to mourn:
Her mother Betty, dead and buried
in an unmarked grave
at Mount Vernon's burial ground for slaves.
No signage allowed; remembrance not required.
"Mulatto" Betty, last name a mystery,
guessed to be in her fifties,
dead from slavery's endless days.

Philadelphia
1796

NO LONGER

For Ona, thought to be twenty-three,
being First Maid had lost its shine.
Her mother and brother, gone.
It was time to reckon with what she'd known
since her Separation Day:
She would work the rest of her life
without pay, never allowed to live
by her wits, do what she wanted,
or go where she wished.
Pretty dresses held no charm
nor did being the Grand Lady's pet
nor feeling like a special slave.

Ona could no longer delude herself
that she was a member of the famous family.

SHOCKS

Granddaughter Eliza shocked
President and Lady Washington
when she announced she would marry
a man twenty years her senior.
Husband-to-be Thomas Law
had returned from India,
White as a snowy day
with two Brown children but
no mother for them or him a wife.
The way he looked at Ona
made her blush, and jealousy flashed
in Eliza's eyes.

Not long after, this news:
the President was retiring!
He and the Grand Lady
would return to Mount Vernon.
If Ona was going to flee,
time was running out.

Then Ona received
a shattering jolt.
Martha Washington told her with a smile
she would give Ona to Eliza
as a wedding gift!

DECISION

Go or stay? Run or suffer?
She was a slave to be given away.
Being a fugitive was for the brave.

The country's Fugitive Slave Law
made her an outlaw if she ran.
Who would hire an outlaw maid?
Being a fugitive was for the brave.

Black freedom fighters
would show her the way.
A White sea captain
would take her aboard.
Being a fugitive was for the brave.
Ona decided.
She was one of the brave.

Philadelphia
May 21, 1796

FREEDOM SEEKER

Ona put a plan in play
to save her from Negro Tom's fate.
She packed small bundles
for someone to carry
one by one
to a freedom fighter's home.

On an evening in May,
as George and Martha sat to dine
Ona walked out of slavery's door
and with her freedom step
changed from the trusted First Maid
to a thief who stole herself.

STOLEN FREEDOM

She hurried to the secret spot
where her clothes were hidden,
waited until the White ship captain
of the *Nancy* and his crew
of free Black sailors were ready to sail.
Smuggled aboard, Ona burrowed
between casks of molasses
and crates of potatoes
as the Delaware River's gentle slaps
turned into the stomach-churning Atlantic
and reached White New Hampshire.

Stolen freedom precious to the slave
is fear in the throat of a Black fugitive.

INGRATITUDE, REWARD

Ona's deception confirmed
what the Grand Lady had long believed:
> *Blacks are so bad*
> *in their nature that they have not*
> *the least gratitude for the kindness*
> *that may be shewed to them.*

The President felt betrayed.
He posted a reward for the capture
of his wife's runaway maid.
Wasn't sure of her age
but knew the value of a human enslaved:
> *ten dollars will be paid*
for the capture of outlaw Ona Judge.

ONEY!

Stolen freedom
spotted in the town square
exposed on a summer market day.
Betsy, a frequent visitor
to the President's House with her father—
Senator John Langdon,

who with George Washington
had signed the Constitution—
spotted the fugitive and shouted
  Oney! Where in the world
  have you come from?
Hearing the name the Washingtons used,
Ona's hands quivered until she summoned
her fugitive's pride.
  Run away, misses.
Astounded by Ona's answer, Betsy said
  And from such an excellent place!
  Why, what could induce you?
  You had a room to yourself
  and only light nice work to do
  and every indulgence.
With more pride, Ona said
before she hurried away:
  Yes, I know, but I want to be free, misses.

Philadelphia
September 1796

A TRIFLING

The President knew where to find
the runaway maid.
He wrote the Portsmouth customs agent
who worked for the government
George Washington controlled.
He apologized for disturbing
the agent with

33

such a trifling occasion
but asked him
    To seize and put on board a Vessel
    bound immediately to this place.

    [Ona] treated more like a child than a Servant.

The agent, now a slave-catcher
did the President's bidding.
He let it be known he needed a maid.
Ona, in need of work, foolishly applied
and soon discovered the trick.

Philadelphia
October 1796

UNFAITHFUL

Ona was not a *child*, but a woman
who had declared herself free
but still felt a tug toward the familiar.
Perhaps the custom agent's discomfort
at his slave-catcher's task
made her take pity, or perhaps
she worried about baby sister Delphy.
(She had no way of knowing
that the Grand Lady had given
the sixteen-year-old to Eliza.)
Or perhaps work in White New Hampshire
for a Black fugitive was as scarce

34

as the pennies in her purse.
Or she needed time
to trick the trickster?
Whatever the reason
Ona bought time
and agreed to return if,
upon Martha Washington's death,
she would be set free.
George Washington—a general,
slaveowner, and President—was dismayed
when he read the agent's letter.
An enslaved servant dared to bargain!
He sent his cold reply.
He would not
> *reward unfaithfulness.*

Portsmouth, New Hampshire
January 14, 1797

LOVE AND MARRIAGE

Neither slave nor free
Ona carved a life in a rented cottage
neither grand as the President's House
nor bleak as a slave cabin.
She could come and go as she pleased
> work for pay
> learn to read
> and marry
> with the blessing of church and law.

Ona and Jack Staines
a free Black merchant marine
married on a cold winter day.
One year later, a baby daughter
soft and sweet, they named her Eliza
and promised she would not grow up to be
a woman sassy and mean.

The law still claimed children
of enslaved mothers were but baby slaves.
It didn't matter if the father was free.
Ona now had a greater fear.
Baby Eliza was an outlaw fugitive too.
Another generation to be enslaved
by the most powerful couple in America.

Mount Vernon
September 1799

TROUBLE

The President and the Grand Lady
had returned to Mount Vernon
with its three hundred slaves,
but when the agent reported
Ona was married and a mother
the Washingtons wanted two more.

Burwell Bassett Jr.
Martha Washington's nephew,

a man we will call Trouble,
knew the way to his rich aunt's heart and purse.
He would journey north and kidnap
the outlaw Ona Judge and baby Eliza.

Portsmouth, New Hampshire
October 1799

DEFIANCE

Ona's basket by the cottage door
held the sewing she had to do
to keep the pennies coming in.
Husband Jack was out at sea.
She had a one-year-old to feed.

Trouble rapped on Ona's door.
Baby Eliza started to cry.
Trouble knocked harder
knowing they were inside.
He hammered with his Fugitive Slave Law's fists
eager to grab his rich aunt's stolen property
and haul them back to Mount Vernon
to keep his dollars flowing in.

Ona threw open the door.
A poker iron propped nearby,
a stitching needle at her side
she stared Trouble in the face.
From the doorway, he told his lie.

His aunt wanted her maid back
and would set her free.
Ona told Trouble what he didn't want to hear:
I am free now.

FREEDOM FIGHTER

Trouble, a dinner guest
at Senator Langdon's house,
spoke as though the Black waiter
serving dinner
had no ears to hear his boast:
Trouble would grab Ona and her daughter
drag them to a waiting ship
return them to Mount Vernon
and be rewarded by his grateful aunt.
The waiter, a slavery freedom fighter,
with the senator's consent
stepped into the crisp night air
and sent Ona a warning.

FLIGHT

Ona Judge pledged:
    she should rather suffer death
    than return to slavery
and threw aside her stitching
    grabbed baby Eliza
    hurried to the nearby stable

hired a driver and his wagon
galloped into freedom's woods.

Later that night Trouble
rapped on Ona's door
banged so hard with his kidnapper's might
the door fell in.
A few miles away Ona and Eliza
stayed safe and warm
in the home of a free Black family.

New Hampshire
1799–1802

FREEDOM'S AIR

George and Martha Washington
went to their graves.
No one else came to reclaim
their runaway maid.
Ona Judge's life was long
and fugitive hard.
For a half-century, without regret,
she eked out a living.
With the love of her husband
and three children, she breathed
impoverished freedom's air
purer than being sold or given away.

THE QUESTION

A reporter asked Ona:
Did she have regrets
for breaking slavery's hold
and grabbing freedom's wing?
He watched amazed as a smile
crisscrossed her crinkled freckled face.
>   *No, I am free, and have,*
>   *I trust, Been made a child of God.*

Yes, bent and spent
living in freedom's poverty
but not by slavery's crush.
Yes, husband Jack long buried at sea
with love for her in his heart.
Yes, children dead and gone
but not sold, their fate unknown.

ONA'S DECLARATION

Ona stitched and sewed,
her once-nimble fingers
withered and aged.
Her sight began to fade.

Thought to be seventy-four,
she opened her eyes no more.
The law called her a fugitive outlaw,
but Ona Judge had declared herself free
and took what others thought was not hers—
Herself.

FREDERICK DOUGLASS

The Day and

The wretchedness of slavery,
and the blessedness of freedom
were perpetually before me.

—Frederick Douglass
1818–1895

AND HARRIET TUBMAN
1818-1913

Night Warriors

*There was one of two things
I had a right to, liberty or death;
if I could not have one,
I would have the other.*

—Harriet Tubman
1822–1913

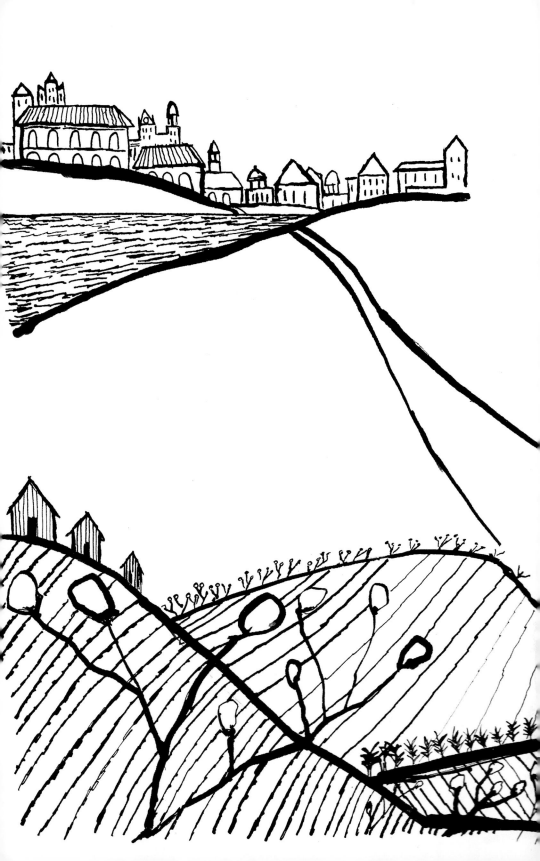

Slavery's Story
1818–1849

THE JOURNEY

Like Ona Judge, two strangers
declared themselves free
when they passed through
Philadelphia eleven years apart.
The spirit that glowed
from Pennsylvania's State House—
where the Declaration of Independence
and the U.S. Constitution were signed—
blazed in Frederick Douglass's
and Harriet Tubman's hearts
as they liberated themselves
and four million more.

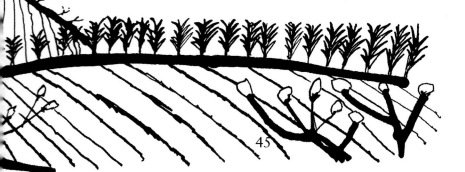

Talbot County, Maryland
February 1818

FREDERICK DOUGLASS

On Maryland's Eastern Shore
Old Master Anthony added a slave child
to his substantial property
as if a wobbly legged foal
or a newborn calf had dropped
on the barnyard ground.

As was the practice of the day
Frederick Augustus Washington Bailey's
birth was not recorded,
but the wise folks at Holme Hill Farm
best remembered it:
Before planting time, 1818,
give or take a year or two.

Old Master sent Frederick's mother
to a farm a half-night's walk away.
Left the child in his grandmother's lap.
His mother Harriet, with no last name,
walked back on rare nights
risked a whipping for an hour visit
with her sleeping baby boy.

HARRIET TUBMAN

Young Master Brodess added a slave child
to his paltry property
as if a nanny goat or piglet
had dropped on the barnyard ground.

As was the practice of the day
Araminta "Minty" Ross's birth
was not recorded, but the wise folks
of Peter's Neck district
along Maryland's Eastern Shore
best remembered it:
Before planting time, 1822,
give or take a year or two.

By the age of three or four
Minty watched her parents
twist in terror's sorrow.
Their sixteen-year-old Mariah
sold to slave traders.
How soon, wondered Rit and Ben,
before their child Minty
would be sold to fatten
Master Brodess's skimpy purse?

Maryland's Eastern Shore
1824

FAMILY

In the year of his sixth harvest
Frederick struggled to keep pace
with his grandmother's grim stride
on their twelve-mile hike
to the Great House Farm
where a stunned and confused Frederick
met his mother's other children.
His grandmother left him
with his brothers and sisters
and vanished into scratchy underbrush.
Another grandchild abandoned
in slavery's brutal cage.

Fed *like so many pigs,*
Frederick, his brother, two sisters,
and a bevy of cousins scooped
corn mush with oyster shells
from a wooden trough.
He slept on the hard clay floor
in the kitchen's dark crawlspace.
On cold nights, he tucked headfirst
inside a dirty corn sack and cried
among the scampering mice.

MEMORY

Around his seventh harvest
Frederick learned of his mother's death.
He faintly remembered her ghostly visits—
the warmth, her sweet and haunting smell.
Of his father he knew even less.
Old folks whispered: his mother
darker than her dark parents;
his father must have been White
given Frederick's color.
Meaning: the son, a child of force.

WHIPPED

One night on the cold clay floor,
screams shook Frederick from his sleep.
No corn sack could muffle
the horrid sounds.
Aunt Hester—fifteen years old—stretched tiptoe
from a bench to a ceiling hook.
Old Master, unmoored from law
and human nature, flaying
Hester's bare brown back
with *a blood-clotted cowskin*
for rejecting his lusty intent.
Each sadistic stroke came
with an unholy call and response:
d . . . d, LASH, b . . . h, LASH.
Oath and lash, a deranged dance
of humiliation and power.

Bucktown, Maryland
1822–1835

FAMILY

Minty's family, again torn apart
in a different way,
yet the pain the same.
Her parents had different masters.
Anthony Thompson owned Ben;
his stepson Ed Brodess owned Rit.
Brodess turned twenty-one,
the legal age to claim what was his:
Rit, Minty, and the other children.
A year later Brodess and his wife
moved to a rundown farm ten miles
up the lane and took Rit and her children,
left Ben to beg for a family visit.

RENTED

On her fifth or sixth planting season,
Minty was rented to a farmer
living by a freshwater swamp.
At night she cried herself to sleep
in a box on the kitchen floor.
Winter days she spent
tending muskrat traps.
The musky pelts brought coins

to the farmer and his wife
and meat for their meager table.
They sent barefooted Minty into cold,
creepy bogs and in no more clothes
than her rough cotton smock
to set the deadly traps.

Soon, sick and measles-spotted,
Minty pleaded with the farmer's wife,
who chose to hear
the whining of a lazy slave
and sent Minty to the swamp
until this feverish child
collapsed and was returned
with a money-back demand.

Now a child of seven or eight
rented once again
to clean house during the day
rock a colicky baby through the night.
Minty struggled to stay awake,
failed to keep the baby content.
The crying woke Miss Susan
who thrashed Minty about the neck and back,
stained her body and soul
in searing welts.

Once when Miss Susan argued
with her husband
Minty helped herself to a lump of sugar.
Rawhide whip in hand, the mistress
chased the sugar thief.

Minty hid in a neighbor's pigsty
wondered if her haste
to taste a sugary sweet
would be worth the days of hunger
and whipping sure to come.

WHY?

A question Minty must have pondered
hiding among the pigs:
How does a penniless child
fly from slavery's cage?
Later she would ask:
>Why should such things be?

A question Frederick must have pondered
curled up in the crawlspace:
How does an orphan child
fly from slavery's cage?
Later he would ask:
>Why are some people slaves and others masters?

Baltimore
1826–1834

TOSSED

Old Master Anthony was dying,
his slaves tossed in the air
to be given away or sold.
Frederick soft-landed
with the master's daughter Lucretia
and her husband Thomas Auld,
who had no need for a young slave and
loaned eight-year-old Frederick
to their two-year-old nephew Tommy
who lived way up in Baltimore.

Tommy's mother Sophia
a first-time slave mistress
her heart not yet hardened
treated Freddy like her Tommy.
As her baby boy learned the alphabet
so did his slave Freddy.
Husband Hugh discovered the crime:
Reading made a child unfit to be enslaved.
Through Sophia's unfrozen heart
Frederick stumbled upon his
pathway from slavery to freedom.

THIEF

Like a thief, the eleven-year-old
Frederick had pried open an unguarded
treasure chest and helped himself
to the riches hidden inside words:
from the Bible left open
on the kitchen table,
from scraps of newspapers blowing
down city streets.
He peppered poor White boys
with questions about words taught
in the school he could not attend.
With money earned from extra errands,
he added another secret jewel
to his pilfered treasury:
The Columbian Orator, a fifty-cent book
on how to speak with elegance
about the place he wanted to reach
with the *vocabulary* of liberation:
freedom, liberty, tyranny, and the rights of man.

STONEHEART

Slavery turned the softest heart
stone hard. Sophia obeyed husband Hugh
and began to see reading made her Freddy
unfit to be a slave.
She scolded the boy when she caught
him in a corner with a book
and a troubled gaze across his face.

In his stolen moments Frederick read
out loud the *vocabulary* of liberation:
    freedom,
    liberty,
    tyranny, and
    the rights of man
each word echoed in the empty room
that he imagined was filled with thousands
he had persuaded to set him free.

Maryland's Eastern Shore
1833

SCHOOL

Frederick's legal owner Thomas Auld,
now a widower and remarried,
had a dispute with his brother Hugh
demanded Frederick's return.
Fifteen, back on the Eastern Shore
Frederick kept his freedom dream
started a Sabbath school.
On Sunday afternoons in the woods
he taught others how to improve their
mind[s] *and heart*[s] *by learning*
to read the sacred scriptures.

Thomas Auld discovered the crime:
esteemed a most dangerous nuisance,
to be instantly stopped.

ANOTHER PIGSTY

Thomas Auld rented Frederick
to Edward Covey to break
his freedom-seeking spirit.
Kicked, beaten, worked like a mule,
Frederick found relief in bottles of tipsy juice
to numb his pain, soothe misery
until in a drunken fog
he stumbled across a field and laid
himself down near a pigsty,
and the pig being out at that time,
crawled into it.
Ashamed, he prayed and promised
no more nights of tipsy juice
no more day-time beatings.
When Covey next attacked,
Frederick grabbed him by the neck
wrestled him to the ground
to a new understanding.
He was enslaved but not a slave.

1836

BETRAYED

Fighting back did not quell
freedom's urge.
With a group of four
Frederick plotted an escape—
more a fantasy than a freedom break:

Sneak to the Chesapeake Bay,
steal a canoe, paddle seventy miles,
slip through slave states Maryland
and Delaware and reach
the free state of Pennsylvania.

Betrayed, exposed, and jailed,
Frederick waited to be sold.
Hungry slave traders circled,
calculated his muscles
into auction block dollars
until Thomas Auld shooed
the vultures away.

The Auld brothers' greed
proved bigger than their family quarrel.
A slave with a trade brought
a lifetime flow of money
greater than a one-time sale.
Frederick was sent back to Baltimore
to learn a caulker's craft,
which keeps ships watertight.

Baltimore
1837

APPRENTICESHIP

In the shipyards, White apprentices
refused to work if a Black apprentice
was taught their trade.

Frederick refused to quit
but could not match
the blows of five or six.
They beat him to a pulp
left him with a mangled eye.
Sophia Auld, her heart moved to pity,
nursed Freddy back to health.
Her husband found another shipyard
where Frederick could learn a caulker's trade.

1838

ANNA

Frederick sharpened his speaking skills
preached now and then at
Bethel African Methodist Episcopal Church
found love and a partner one day
when his eyes left the sermon
and found Anna Murray,
a free woman who could not
read or write but knew her Bible
and right from wrong.

RUN OR STAY

Anna and Frederick planned a life together.
"Run or stay" ricocheted
through Frederick's brain.
If he ran, Anna could follow, she was free.
If caught, he would be sold.
If he stayed and had children
they would be born free
but he could be sold anyway.
If he ran smart, with a plan,
he would be free until caught.
There was no choice.
He would run.

Frederick convinced an old sailor
to sell him his seaman's protection papers
with the American Eagle embossed,
showing he was a Black Jack—
a free and legal seagoing Black.
Anna sewed him a uniform
sold her prized feather-bed mattress
and put running-away money
in Frederick's pocket.
On the first Monday in September
Frederick boarded the Negro car
on the Baltimore–Wilmington train
waved goodbye to Anna

who must have worried:
Would the man she loved
keep his promise or just her money?

Baltimore
October 1838

INSIDE AND OUT

Later, Frederick wrote
how easy it looked on the outside.
The conductor glanced at his papers
accepted him as the free Black sailor
even though he did not resemble
the man described beneath the American Eagle.
Later he wrote of his fear of being caught:
>On the train to Wilmington, Delaware
>On the steamboat to Philadelphia
>On the train to New Jersey
>On the ferry to New York City.

New York City
September 1838

FUGITIVE

On dark and fish-reeking cobblestone streets
Frederick's freedom turned to icy sweat.
No longer enslaved, something worse:
a fugitive outlaw on the run.

I was yet liable to be taken back,
and subjected to all the torture of slavery.
There I was in the midst of thousands,
and yet a perfect stranger; without home,
and without friends.

HARRIET TUBMAN

Bucktown, Maryland
1834–1836

LESSONS

Though not allowed to learn to read
or write, Minty received lessons
that could guide her from slavery's cage:
From a book her mother Rit could not read,
she taught Minty the story of Moses
leading his people out of slavery;
and her father Ben taught her
how to read moss
on the north side of trees,
how to find the North Star in the night sky.

VISIONS

Minty's babysitting and muskrat-
trapping days came to an end.
Tiny, now about fourteen,
she worked like a mule,

planting and harvesting flax—
a stubborn yellow-gray crop
that could be spun into elegant linen
worn by inelegant people.

One afternoon Minty went with the cook
to a dry goods store for some kitchen stuff.
A slave was inside
trying to escape or wanting a say
on how he would spend his day.
His overseer tracked him down.
The hunted man decided to run.
Furious, the overseer heaved
a two-pound weight from the measuring scale
just as Minty stepped through the door
and knocked her into a two-day trance.

PRIVATE CONVERSATIONS

Some thought God showed Minty
things they couldn't see.
Others said she was made crazy
when the flying weight buried
a piece of the rag that had covered
her hair, now lodged in her skull.
But the knock on the head
caused her to see
freedom's road.

Blood seeping down her face,
Minty was back to mule-work in the field.

There were times her mind went blank
in the middle of a sentence
or mid-pull on stalks.
When startled awake
words rushed from her mouth
making others pause and marvel
at Minty's private conversations with God.

1841

LIBERTY OR DEATH

Minty witnessed once again
the shattering sorrow
of her family torn apart.
Georgia slave traders tied her sisters
Linah and Soph in a coffle,
marched them to human flesh markets
deeper south.
Master Brodess, desperate for money
had sold them for four hundred dollars and
showed no remorse when they cried
in *hopeless grief*.
Linah's two daughters, Kessiah and Harriet,
too young for the long and painful trek
were left behind for a future sale.
The sale of her sisters led Minty to pledge:

> *I had a right to liberty or death;*
> *and if I could not have one,*
> *I would have the other.*

MARRIAGE

At twenty-two or -three
Minty married John Tubman,
a free man of color.
Four years before, her father Ben was freed
when thought to be forty-five
as his master had agreed.
Ben worked, saved twenty dollars,
and bought Rit's freedom.
Perhaps Minty had a similar hope,
John would save and buy her freedom.

It must have been pure love for John
to take a wife who was enslaved,
which meant their children
would never be free.
Minty showed her love
stitched a marriage quilt
and moved into John's cabin.

1848

THIEVERY

Much of Minty's life remains a mystery.
How she learned of the theft
of her mother's freedom
is unknown to this day.

Perhaps it came in a star-clustered vision
or maybe she'd heard it as a slave-yard tale
the kind to pass the day
to keep the blues at bay.
Or perhaps because husband John
had yet to save enough to buy her freedom
Minty decided to free herself.
Believed to be twenty-six
she hired a lawyer who burned away
the fog that hid a lie.
The truth:
When Rit, Minty's mother, was about nine
her first master willed her
to his granddaughter, Mary.
The will said when Rit turned forty-five
she would be set free.
The same for her future children
when they reached forty-five.
But Mary violated her grandfather's will,
refused to free Rit and sold her children.
Mary whispered the secret to her son
Edward Brodess, who continued
his mother's deceit, kept Rit enslaved
until she was over fifty,
sold more of her children
when he needed money.

PRAYER AND FEAR

Months of praying for her master
to repent his deceitful, thieving ways
brought no change.
Minty offered a different prayer:
Lord, if you ain't never going to change
that man's heart, kill him.

In a bevy of foul curses
Edward Brodess died.
The master's death tossed up
the fate of his slaves
to be given away or sold
by Widow Brodess with debts to pay
eight children to feed.
Fear began to spread.
Georgia slave traders on their way.

September 17, 1849

TRIO

With slave traders coming
Minty had to go!
Husband John said no.
He wasn't willing to leave
the only place he'd known.
He would stay and pray his wife

would not be sold.
Minty couldn't wait
for his change of heart.
John may pray but she would run.
Her brothers Ben and Harry,
also at risk of being sold,
joined Minty.
The trio headed for the door.

FROZEN COURAGE

Three weeks in the woods,
hunger and cold
froze her brothers' courage.
Minty wanted to keep to her vision
but they could not see what she saw.
They'd rather take a lash or two
and stand on the auction block
than be torn apart by dogs
or shot by slave hunters
meaner than their canines.
Out of brotherly love, Ben and Harry
dragged Minty back to husband John.

RUN OR STAY

"Run again or stay" ricocheted
through Minty's brain.
If she ran, husband John could follow.
He was a free Black man.
If caught, she would be sold.
If she stayed and had children
they would be born slaves
but she could be sold anyway,
her children too.
If she ran smart with a plan
she would be free until caught.
There was no choice.
Minty would run.

Husband John warned:
Run again and I'll tell.
Minty waited until he began
to huff and snore
gathered her marriage quilt
left her free husband and unfree brothers.

LIBERTY

Minty caught the Underground Railroad,
the secret network without tracks or trains
with many conductors and stations
for hiding a slave on the run.

Her ride was a 120-mile walk
of courage and grit.
Slave-catchers with guns and dogs
could do her great harm.
She spent her days in the woods
or friendly barns
spent her nights walking under
the North Star's light or feeling for moss
on the north side of trees.
Minty ran smart and kept her promise:
She would have
liberty or death, one or the other.

Philadelphia
October 1849

STRANGE LAND

Minty used her mother's full name
Harriet.
Hoping they would be together again
she kept her husband's name
with the faith he would wake and follow.
Harriet Tubman was no longer a slave
but someone worse—
a fugitive outlaw alone in a city
jammed with noise and loud folks
in a rush to be someplace
or with someone they loved.
She had neither friend
nor spot to rest her drowsy head.

There was no one to welcome me
to the land of freedom.
I was a stranger in a strange land;
and my home, after all,
was down in Maryland;
because my father, my mother,
my brothers, and sisters, and friends were there.
But I was free and they should be free.

Freedom
1838–1863

Stand-ins
Frederick and Harriet:
together and separate
two pieces of property
stand-ins for millions
who'd come and gone since 1619—
two hundred and thirty years—
a human herd corralled
behind a wicked fence
as wide as the country
and cruel as history's many wrongs.

Harriet and Frederick:
separate and together
two pieces of property
bruised and abused
within an inch of being sold
committed a crime
like Ona Judge and many more
who ran for freedom
became fugitive outlaws
in America's Slavery Story
on their way to Freedom's Story.

New York City
1838

PROMISE

Frederick Bailey
toil-worn and whip-scarred fugitive
a slave on the run
at liberty but not free
in need of a place to hide
and a name for disguise.
New York City's Underground Railroad conductor
warned: Keep running.
Before he ran, Frederick had a promise
to keep. Anna soon joined him
and they did what Maryland slaves couldn't—
legally married. Then they ran together.

New Bedford, Massachusetts

OLD SCORN

As Mr. and Mrs. Johnson
to disguise their identity
Frederick and Anna raced
to Massachusetts, a state
that had outlawed slavery years before.
In New Bedford, a whaling center

74

a fierce freedom-loving town
with ships in need of caulking
the new couple found a new life
and an old scorn—RACE!
Anna did domestic work for wealthy
White families.
And White caulkers refused to work
with Black Frederick.
The husband and wife
had to learn to live
in the northern mixture
of freedom-loving and anti-Black.

1839

DOUGLASS

New Bedford had twenty-three Johnsons
a name too popular
at least half of them marked *C* for *colored*
increasing the risk of being *captured.*
Frederick chose a second new name, Douglas
from a Scottish novel
doubled the *S*
made it his own:
Frederick Douglass.

The double-*S* fugitive rolled whale oil barrels
from ships to storage houses
along smelly Rose Alley.

At night he read
thought about how to end
being a fugitive outlaw
how to achieve all he was capable.
Sunday mornings to Sunday evenings
he practiced his oratorical skills—
a pathway to freedom—
as a licensed preacher at the
African Methodist Episcopal Zion Church.

1839–1849

FAMILY

Anna and Frederick grew to more than two:
First came Rosetta, 1839;
a year later, Lewis; Frederick Junior in '42;
Charles in '44; and in '49, their fifth child, Annie.
Living quarters grew tight.
Frederick needed to grow as fast.
He studied, pushed, and climbed
a ladder built from words and ideas
until he stood on stages in northern states
and across the Atlantic.
Slavery was the text, freedom the script.

THE WARRIOR'S VOICE

On the sail to Nantucket Island
to an abolitionist meeting
sixty miles away
being Black kept Frederick
on the windswept deck
rather than in the warm cabin
where the White passengers sat.
On the stage, standing six foot two
muscular, handsome
his African hair a young lion's mane
Frederick rose and told his story
peeled away slavery's mask
bared the scars of greed and cruelty—
told of the ill-fed, poorly clothed,
and of sexual violence,
families ripped apart for profit.
Listeners sat dazed.
This Black warrior's voice,
his polished words
were something seldom heard.

To the spellbound abolitionist leader
William Lloyd Garrison
this warrior could add force to the cause,
the end of slavery.
Frederick Douglass could give

northern Whites a novelty
the raw power of a former slave
who knew firsthand enslavement's brutality.

Garrison hired Frederick for his New England
Anti-Slavery Society to tell the story
of American bondage, and by his presence,
show why slavery was wrong.

Pendleton, Indiana
September 1843

HECKLED

Belief in White superiority
and Black inferiority was buried too deep
to be uprooted like an unwanted weed.
Racial arrogance and custom
Shunned the idea of equality.

Frederick traveled from town to town
and with eloquent words told the story
of the evils of American slavery.
A story most didn't want to hear
but were eager to show the North
was not free of color prejudice.
He was forced to ride in the train car
behind the engine, its air clogged
in coal smoke.
He was denied places to eat or sleep

and his speeches were interrupted
with rancid heckles and rotten eggs.

William Lloyd Garrison
preached moral suasion—
that words alone could persuade those
who believed in slavery
to renounce their belief.

Moral suasion was tested and failed
on a September day in 1843.
When Frederick rose to speak
in Indiana, eggs hit first,
then a club-swinging mob rushed the platform
leaving him with a broken hand.
Two days later, bandaged and bruised,
he took the stage
protected not by moral suasion
but abolitionists' guns and pitchforks.

1845

THE NARRATIVE

Many refused to believe
Frederick had ever been a slave.
If slavery was as bad as he claimed,
there couldn't be such an eloquent
a speaker as he.
Charges of fraud led him to write

his autobiography:
> *Narrative of the Life of Frederick Douglass.*

To answer doubt that an uneducated fugitive
could write a book, he added the subtitle
> *Written by Himself.*

The book caused a sticky problem:
Writing it to prove his enslavement
told the Auld brothers, his owners,
where to find their runaway.
It showed why slavery was called
a "peculiar institution."
To prove he was once enslaved
he had to risk being re-enslaved.
Frederick had to escape again.

United Kingdom
1846

STEERAGE

On the *Cambria* crossing the sea
the fugitive sailed with a trunkful
of his *Narrative* to sell at anti-slavery meetings
in Ireland, England, Scotland, and Wales.
He would bring attention
to the American contradiction:
Though it claimed to be the land of the free,
four million of its people were enslaved.
Even on the ocean, there would be no break
from those who thought him less.

His first-class ticket was not honored.
Frederick was forced into steerage,
below the waterline.

PRIVILEGE

The ship's captain, in a twinge of guilt
or wanting to entertain his passengers
on the next-to-last day of the long voyage
asked the orator to give a talk on being enslaved.
A privilege to speak granted to a fugitive?
Some passengers rose in alarm.
From their first-class berths
down the promenade deck
they shouted threats to throw overboard
the man who did not know he was still a slave.
Frederick braced himself
ready to toss into the Atlantic
the first to reach him.
The captain called for order and chains
for the men drunk on rum and slavery.

United Kingdom
1846–1847

SEA MOB

News of the onboard standoff against
salt water mobocrats
buzzed through England when the ship arrived.

The fugitive abolitionist became the star
that anti-slavery advocates had to hear.
For eighteen months he spoke
harangued and cajoled
mocked slavery and those arrogant
enough to own a human being.
Here, above the color line
he ate, traveled, slept where he chose
and could afford
but he longed for Anna and his children
for home and family.
No amount of applause or admiration
soothed the isolation and despair.

England
April 1846

RANSOM

The English Anti-Slavery Society
raised £150 sterling
to buy Frederick's freedom.
Master Auld was delighted with
seven hundred dollars and eleven cents
for property eight years missing.
Some leaders said it
weakened their cause
when English friends paid
a kidnapper's ransom
for Frederick's freedom.

These leaders had neither been enslaved
nor forced to leave their families.

Frederick could return to America
without fear of being returned to slavery.
Again he sailed aboard the *Cambria*
a free man, but still someone to scorn.
His first-class ticket was not honored.
He had to sail in steerage
below the waterline.

Rochester, New York
December 1847

THE NORTH STAR

Frederick settled in upstate New York
not far from the Canadian border.
Made his family home a station stop
on the Underground Railroad.
With a gift of £500 sterling—
more than twenty-five hundred dollars—
from Irish and British friends
he started a newspaper, the *North Star*.
His paper would light the way
of the Underground Railroad.

*Cape May, New Jersey
1850–1852*

DREAMS

Unable to read or write
did not mean Harriet had no
skills or smarts.
She could think and plot
as she cooked and cleaned
in a house here, a home there
a hotel anywhere.
Rich folks on Cape May
thought their Black maid strange,
falling asleep while standing
waking in a jumble of mumbles—
a half-crazed vision of a land
called Freedom.
They had Harriet all wrong.
With each cup of milk and stir of an egg
her plotting went from dough to bread
to a dream of setting loved ones free
and a place safe for her freed mother and father
and even husband John.

BLOODHOUNDS

Slaveholders could take it no more!
Frederick Douglass's thundering words
stripped away the fancy gloss
that claimed slaves were loved like children
who from time to time needed discipline
to make them better behaved.

Harriet Tubman's escape
was one too many of the misbehaving
running for liberty.
Congress, with its love for slavery,
dammed the misbehavers' northern surge.

Slaveowners' allies in Congress
passed the *second* Fugitive Slave Act,
a law with sharper teeth, greater bite
than the act George Washington
had signed in 1793
and Ona Judge defied in '96.
Fugitives and their abolitionist allies
called it the Bloodhound Law
for making every White a slave-catcher
every Black, whether fugitive or free,
prey for kidnapping.
Anyone who helped a slave escape
faced a thousand-dollar fine
and six months in jail.

For fugitives accused
no jury trial required
self-defense not allowed.
The judges appointed to speed things up
got ten dollars
if they found the accused a runaway;
but only five
for ruling the other way.

Maryland's Eastern Shore
1851

RESCUE

Word reached Harriet of troubles back home.
Widow Brodess, heavily in debt,
would put Harriet's niece Kessiah
and her two children on the auction block.
Harriet took down her dream jar
counted the coins
tucked a pistol under her dress
rode a train hunched low in second-class
hid her dented forehead under a floppy hat
the look of a harmless slave
freed because of old age, or mental decline.
Harriet, young and strong,
on her way to save two generations.

HER PLAN

Harriet never revealed how
she rescued her niece.
She gave credit to God
and the visions in her head.
How long she waited in Baltimore
she didn't say but knew the day
Kessiah and her children stepped
onto the auction block.

Kessiah's freeborn husband
John Bowley, a Chesapeake Bay fisherman
light in color because his father was White
attracted no attention bidding at the auction
controlled his anger as other buyers
with their hands
examined his wife and children.

The bids rose higher
for the brown-skinned mother
as if she were a Plymouth Rock hen
with two chicks who could produce more
for the owner's chicken pen.
Sold to the highest bidder.
Another family broken apart
or so the seller thought.
But John Bowley, husband and father,
made the highest bid.

LIBERTY

Seller left to lunch and drink.
Harriet's plan underway.
John Bowley led Kessiah, James,
and Araminta to the holding pen
where they would stay until the auctioneer
finished his lunch and drink.
John led his wife and children
to a nearby abolitionist's safe house.
The auctioneer returned,
called for his money, but John was gone.
Later that night he and his family
sailed up the Choptank River
to the choppy Chesapeake Bay
to Baltimore, where Aunt Harriet Tubman
led them north to Libertyland.

September 1851

HUSBAND JOHN

No matter how many she brought north
one still missing was husband John.
Harriet took a bolder step.
Carrying a man's suit, she boarded
a Baltimore-bound train
then walked to a spot near their old cabin
sent word of her arrival.

Historians are unsure if the suit
she carried was for John or her disguise
but they know Harriet didn't use
her pistol for his betrayal.
John had taken another wife.

We may think the brave don't cry.
We can feel the sadness
a broken heart holds inside.

Rochester, New York
December 1851

WARRIOR QUEEN

The midnight knock
on Frederick's door
quiet and frantic
came from a small woman with eleven
runaways in need of rest and food.
Frederick took them in:
> *It was the largest number*
> *I ever had at any one time.*

When they left, the fugitives
huddled behind their warrior queen
to continue beyond the reach
of the Fugitive Slave Act.
Harriet Tubman and Frederick Douglass

had not met before that night.
He was free, she was not
and fame had put a price on her head.

MOSES

Harriet made more than ten,
fewer than fifteen missions
back to Slaveryland.
She snatched and stole,
steered, and saved nieces,
nephews, brothers, their girlfriends,
her parents and strangers
but not husband John
making her way through woods and swamps
risking her life to rescue about seventy—
the true number we'll never know.
With a price on her head,
Harriet Tubman guided
fugitives from the *hopeless grief*
she experienced when her sisters were sold.

Fearless trips by train, boat, foot, or cart
Harriet bent like an elderly slave
pockets heavy with abolitionists' coins,
her pistol, and a sachet of magic herbs
to stop babies in the middle of a cry
when slave-catchers rode by.

She led them to Canada,
out of reach of the Bloodhound Law.
Maryland slaveowners posted
a reward for the woman
some called Moses.

Harriet, the night warrior
and Underground Railroad conductor
could claim without exaggeration
I never ran my train off the track
And I never lost a passenger.

FREDERICK DOUGLASS

Corinthian Hall
Rochester, New York
July 5, 1852

CELEBRATION

The day after America's seventy-sixth birthday party,
Frederick Douglass explained what is
    "The Meaning of July Fourth for the Negro."
His answer struck like lightning and singed ears.
But first he paid homage to the founders:
    Fellow Citizens, I am not wanting in respect
    for the fathers of this republic. The signers
    of the Declaration of Independence were brave men.
    They were great men, too—great enough to give
    frame to a great age.

Then Frederick Douglass scorched
the pageantry of the Fourth of July:
> *Whether we turn to the declarations of the past,*
> *or to the professions of the present, the conduct*
> *of the nation seems equally hideous and revolting.*
> *America is false to the past, false to the present,*
> *and solemnly binds herself to be false to the future.*

Washington, D.C.
March 6, 1857

HARRIET AND DRED

The Supreme Court of the United States
ruled against another Harriet
and her husband, Dred Scott.
They'd sued their master's widow
because her army doctor husband
had taken them from Missouri
where slavery was *allowed,* to Illinois
and the Wisconsin Territory
where slavery was *disallowed.*
The master died, and Harriet and Dred
sought their freedom because of the years
they'd lived where slavery was forbidden.
The court's decision startled
Harriet Tubman and Frederick Douglass
when they learned, the Scotts
would remain enslaved.
The U.S. Supreme Court ruled that

Black Americans
were not intended to be included under the word
"citizen" in the Constitution . . .

St. Catharines, Ontario, Canada
April 1858

JOHN BROWN

White and willing to die for the slave,
John Brown was deemed crazy.
The fierce abolitionist
outraged by the Supreme Court's
Dred Scott decision
asked Harriet Tubman
to be his general in a slave rebellion.
Harriet listened, rocked on her porch
smoked her corncob pipe, admired
what the old man asked:
help bring slavery to its knees.
Without sharing when or where
he said his men would steal
an arsenal of army rifles
free those locked in slavery's cage
and lead them into the hills.

SERPENT VISION

Harriet continued to rock
until she floated into a trance
and God showed her a serpent
with terrifying eyes and flicking tongue
which rose from rocks and wrapped itself
around John Brown's legs.
An angry crowd crawled
from beneath the rocks
and beat him with their sticks.
Harriet knew John Brown's fate
months before the hangman's noose
coiled around his neck.

FREDERICK DOUGLASS

Chambersburg, Pennsylvania
August 1859

DISASTER

John Brown and Frederick Douglass
met in a rock quarry
near the Maryland state line.
Brown believed that God commanded
him to ignite a slave revolt.
Douglass warned:
It would be disastrous
to try such a thing.

John Brown with sword and gun
wanted to die for the slave.
Frederick Douglass with pen and voice
chose to live for the slave.

Philadelphia
October 18, 1859

TRAPPED

News of the Harpers Ferry raid
blistered the telegraph wires.
The death trap Frederick warned of
had caught John Brown
and his army of twenty-one.
Frederick, thought to be
behind John Brown's arsenal raid,
was now a wanted man.

He fled to Great Britain
a fugitive once again.
Four months into his stay
a telegram tore open his heart.
Ten-year-old daughter Annie was dead.
Outlaw or not, Frederick left for home.
The trip was long
his sorrow deep and grave.
Annie buried without his goodbye.
As if to mock his fleeing, the government
claimed no interest in his arrest.

Charles Town, Virginia
December 2, 1859

THE GALLOWS

Harriet's vision of John Brown's fate
sprang true when hundreds
of U.S. Army soldiers gasped.
The trapdoor under Brown's feet
snapped open.
His corpse swung beneath the gallows floor.

Troy, New York
April 1860

BROTHERS

Before Harriet Tubman traveled to Boston
to speak at an abolitionist meeting
in spite of the reward for her capture
posted from Baltimore to New York,
she ignored the bounty
stopped in Troy, New York, for a visit
and landed in the middle of a fight.

The Bloodhound Law had sniffed out
Charlie Nalle, a Virginia fugitive,
handcuffed him in a story
stranger than fiction.

96

His master, his younger half brother,
hauled him before a commissioner
who could earn ten dollars if he found
Charlie a fugitive.
Judgment came swift and tidy:
defendant was declared his brother's property.
They had the same father
but their different mothers
made one a master, the other his slave.

THE BID

Handcuffed Charlie was brought
from the courthouse
into a waiting crowd.
One group calling out the price
they'd pay for his freedom
another group urging his brother
to keep him enslaved.
The bid rose as fast as a summer fever,
spiked at twelve hundred dollars.
The master, surprised by his brother's value
demanded three hundred more.
Harriet's bid came sharp and hard:
she jumped on a deputy's back
fought to free the prisoner.
One group rushed to join her
the other rushed to pull her back.
Harriet, knocked to the ground,
rose again and charged back into the melee.
Twenty times the prisoner was taken

twenty times he was recovered
until Harriet grabbed Charlie
shoved her bonnet on his head
led him away while rescuers, officers,
and slavery supporters battled.
Harriet shouted a curse that gave poor
Charlie a scare:
Drag him to the river! Drown him!
But don't let them have him!

ACROSS THE RIVER

The half-conscious Charlie
was pulled and pushed
to the riverbank where Harriet
flung him into a waiting rowboat.
But on the other side of the Hudson River
he was arrested again.
Harriet and her rescue team
crossed the river by the next ferry
learned where Charlie was held
headed to the building
where deputies were duty bound to shoot.
Over fallen bodies Harriet jumped
and others too
burst open the door
broke the law
snatched the fugitive
from the bloodhound's maw.

ANOTHER RISK

Harriet saw the splintering in the land
smelled the scent of war looming in the rift
heard the North ask—Was not allowing
Black slaves in the western territories
worth White lives in a civil war?
Heard the South's cocksure answer
YES! Who else would clear the land
and plant the crops?

A private question gnawed at Harriet's heart,
three of her family still enslaved—
her youngest sister Rachel
and Rachel's children
Angerine and Benjamin.
The last of her family she could save
before the storm of war rained blood.
Friends asked, why take another risk?
Yet she took the train south
from Baltimore, made her way on foot
shivering through a snowy night
on Maryland's Eastern Shore.
The news was colder.
Rachel was dead,

her children, thirteen and eleven,
sold to different plantations.
Harriet refused to surrender
to the cruelty of slavery.
She led another family
of runaways to freedom.

November 1860

THEIR LAND

Blood and thunder in the air.
Harriet and Frederick lived in a land
where their enslavement was the law.
They lived in a land
where if they ran, they could be caught
and re-enslaved.
They lived in a land
where they could not be citizens.
They lived in a land
where if they fought for their rights
they would dance like John Brown
beneath the gallows floor.
There was but one way to change
the land where they lived:
the blood and thunder of civil war.

The Civil War
1861–1865

Springfield, Illinois
November 1860

ABRAHAM LINCOLN

A tall lanky man who hid
his wise and reflective mind
behind a cloak of silly country stories
became President of the United States
with a Constitution that prevented him
from abolishing slavery.
Nothing in the document kept him
from arguing that taking slaves
into western territories not yet states
was not the founders' intent.
It was an argument that both sides
decided could be best settled
in a winner-take-all fight.

Charleston, South Carolina
April 12, 1861

SECESSION

South Carolina left the Union
followed by ten other states.
Twenty-four Union states remained
and the two sides argued
about the right to secede.
The argument turned violent
when cannon fire and smoky fog

covered a Union fort
in Charleston Harbor.
One side wanted to build
an ocean-to-ocean empire
from the sweat of slaves.
The other side wanted
to leave slavery where it was
but not a mile more.
Frederick, Harriet, and folks
who thought like them wanted
slavery buried in its ancient grave.

Spring 1861

DISAPPOINTMENT

Abraham Lincoln's army rejected
Black men eager to join
the Union cause.
The idea of Blacks killing White rebels
offended Northern sensibility.
Harriet repeated her private conversation:
>   *God won't let master Lincoln beat the South*
>   *until he does the right thing.*
Frederick warned it was madness:
>   *Men in earnest don't fight*
>   *with one hand, when they might fight with two.*

Beaufort, South Carolina
Spring 1862

THE SPY

Civilian volunteers were needed
to care for the wounded
and teach former slaves
how to live in freedom.
Harriet raised her hand
boarded a government ship
bound for South Carolina
where Union camps overflowed
with slave refugees.
There was much to learn
about the enemy's strength
from the just-freed slaves
if they would only share.
But they were unsure
of White Union soldiers
and refused to tell what they knew.
Harriet listened, coaxed,
and gained their trust and information
about the Confederates' locations and numbers.
She ventured into the swamps
and woods, scouting, and spying
and returned to camp to share
what she'd learned.
The battle-tried officers were amazed

at how this little Black woman
could sneak onto plantations
bribe overseers, and confirm
what the refugees had told her.

Washington, D.C.
January 1, 1863

EMANCIPATION

On New Year's Day, Abraham Lincoln
signed the Emancipation Proclamation:
declared slaves in Confederate states free.
The Constitution prevented
him from freeing slaves
in Harriet and Frederick's Maryland
and the other Union slave states:
Delaware, Kentucky, and Missouri.

Black men could now join the war.
Frederick recruited Black soldiers
for the Union Army while Harriet
continued to scout and spy
for the Union cause.

Beaufort, South Carolina
January 1, 1863

JUBILEE

Former slaves in the Port Royal
Union Army camp called it Jubilee Day.
A former slaveowner
read the Emancipation Proclamation.
The crowd sang "My Country, 'Tis of Thee,"
but Harriet refused to sing.
Her people in Maryland
remained enslaved.
She would wait for the day
when the Union did what it
demanded of the Confederates:
Free its slaves and let her people go!

Boston
March–May 1863

FATHER'S WORRIES

Frederick helped recruit the first
northern regiment of Black soldiers,
the 54th Massachusetts Infantry.
His son Lewis was a sergeant major.
Proud father watched the regiment's
farewell parade in Boston,

rode on the tugboat that pulled his son's ship
to the ocean before it sailed
for southern battlefields.

RIVER RAID

South Carolina, the first to break
from the United States, became the first
Confederate state hit by the hard punch
of their former slaves.
Their slaves had fled to Union lines
and returned in blue uniforms
sparkling with eagle buttons
and heavy musket rifles.

Harriet, on the deck of the *John Adams*
as it made its way up the Combahee River,
watched the men she'd helped
when they escaped and made
their way ragged and hungry
to the Beaufort Union Army camp.
These same men stood proud and tall
as the Second South Carolina Volunteers
readied themselves to do what war required—
attack and destroy.

REVENGE

For two centuries their ancestors
had made their masters fat and rich.
In pent-up revenge, the former slaves
now Union soldiers, burned granaries,
barns, grand plantation houses,
and flooded freshwater rice fields
in salty ocean water.

Harriet stood on the deck of the Union ship
and might have rubbed the back
of her neck, remembering the lashings
for a lump of sugar
and letting a colicky baby cry.
No doubt her thoughts turned sour
when she thought of her stolen sisters
as hundreds and hundreds of slaves
waded into the Combahee River
to board two overcrowded ships.
More than seven hundred and fifty
made it, but hundreds more were left behind
for the returning masters' revenge.

WHAT HARRIET SAW

Harriet watched as Sergeant Major
Lewis Douglass and the Massachusetts 54th
sprinted toward an impregnable Confederate fort
at the end of a narrow sand spit.
She shuddered as free Black men
and White officers gallantly ran
into the cannon fire.
And then we saw the lightning
and that was the guns;
and then we heard the thunder
and that was the big guns;
and then we heard the rain falling,
and that was drops of blood falling;
and when we came to get in the crops,
it was the dead that we reaped.

THE HARVEST

Two hundred and seventy-three
of the 54th Massachusetts Infantry
fell before Harriet's eyes,
Lewis Douglass, severely wounded.
His father now racked
between pride and doubt.
He had urged his sons Lewis and Charles
to join the fight. Now Lewis suffered
in a Union Army hospital for Black soldiers.
In that hospital, Harriet soothed the foreheads
of the brave. She was the comforter and confessor,
sister and nurse as the wounded suffered,
called for their mothers before they healed or died.
Lewis lived, but most died in neglected agony.
[E]arly every morning I'd get a big chunk of ice,
I would, and put it in a basin, and fill it with water;
then I'd take a sponge and begin.
First man I'd come to, I'd thrash away the flies,
and they'd rise, they would, like bees round a hive.
Then I'd begin to bathe their wounds,
and by the time I'd bathed off three or four,
the fire and heat would have melted the ice
and made the water warm, and it would be
as red as clear blood.

GIANTS

Frederick Douglass and Abraham Lincoln,
an only-in-America pair
unlikely in any other land,
climbed from poverty by brains and grit.
Each wanted victory,
one to save the Union,
the other to save freedom.

The President needed more men
if his side was going to win.
Frederick had urged free Black men,
including his sons, to join the Union
Army because:
We can get at the throat
of treason and slavery . . .
The War Department promised
equal pay, unheard of in its day,
but refused it once the Black soldiers
were behind enemy lines
and had no way home.

DOUBLE WAR

Black soldiers were at the bottom
of the Union ladder.
The idea of a White private saluting
a Black officer was beyond imagination.
Frederick went to see President Lincoln
who greeted him with a smile and firm hand
and would later call him friend.
The two giants discussed equal pay and Black officers.
Lincoln promised he would investigate—
a politician's way of saying you're right
but the time not. Reelection was coming soon
and Lincoln was likely to lose.
Equal pay and Black officers
would cost him White votes.
The 54th soldiers fought and died
for eighteen months without pay
for the privilege of saving the Union.
Their sacrifice helped turn
the Civil War from a draw to victory.

Washington, D.C.
April 15, 1865

TOSSED AGAIN

The myth of race too strong
to be contained by victory.
The threat that former slaves
would become legal equals
sent another casualty to his grave.
The loss shook Frederick's soul
and made Harriet regret
she had refused to meet
Abraham Lincoln.
The President's murder tossed
Black future in the air—
would former slaves remain free
or be re-enslaved?

THE AFTERMATH

The cost of the Civil War moldered
in hundreds of thousands of graves—
the price paid for the victory
enshrined in the Thirteenth Amendment—
the end of American slavery.
But words on a sacred document
were not powerful enough
to change Americans' belief
in the myth of race.
Within a decade the free
were once again unfreed.

Hundreds of thousands of families grieved
the cost of the Civil War—
the price paid for the victory
enshrined in the Fourteenth Amendment—
equal protection from the law.
But words on a sacred document
were not powerful enough
to change Americans' belief
in the myth of race.
New laws could not stop the burning rage
Whites inflicted to keep the freed unfree.

The Civil War had shattered
hundreds of southern cities and towns—
the price paid for only half the victory

granted in the Fifteenth Amendment—
Black men's right to vote.
But words on a sacred document
were not powerful enough
to change Americans' belief
in the myth of race and gender.

Auburn, New York
1869

DAY AND NIGHT WARRIORS

Being unable to write
did not stop Harriet
from telling her story.
A friend pressed it on paper for us
to remember her victories over
the power of slavery.
This small Black woman of uncommon courage
told how she tried to right the wrongs
that had devastated her family.
Frederick Douglass added his words of support
with a message at the front of the book:
Most that I have done . . .
in the service of our cause
has been in public . . .
You on the other hand have
labored in a private way.
I have wrought in the day—
You in the night.

FREEDOM

Death took the warriors, eighteen
years apart, and scattered their spirits
in cosmic dust for storytellers
to catch and press onto pages like these.

Frederick and Harriet lie in graves
in chilly upstate New York
relics of long-ago births
from different mothers named Harriet
on Maryland's warmer Eastern Shore—
born four years and sixty miles apart.

Frederick lies in Rochester's
Mount Hope Cemetery
under a headstone as prominent as his life.
Sixty-five miles distant, Harriet rests
in Auburn's Fort Hill under a granite
headstone as modest as she lived.

ANGELS OF FAIRNESS

On parallel paths, the day and night warriors
rescued the unfree
and fought for Union victory
but were unable to pull
Justice's sword from the Rock of Unfairness.
They left it for warriors who would follow
to pull the shining blade
and slay the monster of racial hate.

The once-enslaved
half-starved children
born among the oyster beds
and muskrat swamps
of Maryland's Eastern Shore
showed the world
the natural thirst for Freedom,
Liberty, and Justice.
The Angels of Fairness threw open
their arms and welcomed
Frederick Douglass and Harriet Tubman
into the Great Hall of American Memory.

PERSONAL HISTORY

When I was fifteen
Emmett Till
a boy near my age
spent summers with his people
in a poor Mississippi town
with a promising name, Money.

On an August night, two White men
as poor as the town
paid a visit to his great-uncle's shack
and dragged Emmett into the moonlit
woods for a festival of gore.

I spent my summers with my people
in a small Missouri town
with a frightening Southern name, Sedalia.
My hot black nights were haunted
knowing Emmett and I were of a race
and age that neither family nor police
could protect from a night of moonlit rage.

PART II

1862-1968

Freedom and Justice

IDA B. WELLS
1862-1931

The Reason Why

*The way to right wrongs
is to turn the light of truth upon
them.*

—Ida B. Wells

FREEDOM'S CHILD

Frederick and Harriet fought
to end American slavery
and nudged the country forward.
The Civil War stranded four million
Black refugees on liberty's rocky road.
In Mississippi, Ida B. Wells
a first-generation freedom child
took her steps whether
the country was ready or not.

Memphis, Tennessee
May 4, 1884

THE LADY

The proper Miss Wells
took a seat in the Ladies' Car
smoothed her newly purchased skirt
adjusted her big hat
settled back for a weekend free
from teaching out-of-slavery's children
in a colored country school.
As the C&O train clickety-clacked out of town
the proud Black teacher
with exaggerated fanfare
flapped open the afternoon paper.

The sullen conductor studied her ticket
shook his head, continued down the aisle
returned with two others
locked in memories of when the world was White.
Nearly two decades since the Civil War
not enough time to accept
their world turned upside down.
A former slave in the Ladies' Car?

COAL DUST

The conductor ordered the proper Miss Wells
to the smoker behind the engine
where fumes and coal dust spewed

and White men sipping pocketed booze
chatted up terrified colored women
while Black men looked the other way.

Miss Wells refused to move,
shoved her thirty-cent ticket
under the conductor's nose.
Slavery nearly twenty years dead!
Outraged, the men grabbed her arm
in a three-against-one show
of manly strength.
The less-than-proper lady
slammed her feet against the seat
braced for a tug-of-war
clawed and fought
and tiger-bit a foul-tasting hand.
The former slave who didn't know her place
was hauled to the smoker
where leering eyes
greeted the proud and proper lady
with her torn sleeves and rumpled hat.

Memphis, Tennessee
1884–1887

NATURAL LAW

Ida B. Wells knew her rights and sued.
A judge startled White Memphis,
awarded Ida five hundred dollars.
One newspaper headline giggled at the horror:

What It Cost to Put a Colored Teacher
in a Smoking Car!
Then a feverish fear began to spread:
Could former slaves believe they're equal?
Another newspaper reassured
that could never be. After all it was
the law of nature for whites
to rule over blacks.

The C&O Railroad fought back.
In a curious display of legalese
the Tennessee Supreme Court
discerned that passenger Wells was
     a mulatto
the Spanish word for mule—
a crossbreed between female horse
and male donkey—a White ancestor
lurked in her family tree
making Ida less than a lady.
These judges agreed
the smoker was the mulatto's place
and overturned the verdict.
Equality could never be.
They punished Ida even more,
fined her two hundred dollars
for the troubles she caused.

SLAVERY'S NEXT OF KIN

In 1865, when the states ratified
the Thirteenth Amendment of the U.S. Constitution,
American slavery came to an end,
but words in this exalted document
did not amend what most held dear:
one race was superior to all others.
Slavery may have been dead
but when the Confederacy lost the war
slavery's next of kin was born:
Jim Crow segregation.
Tennessee made it illegal for Blacks
to ride in first-class or the Ladies' Car.

Jim Crow, craze of make-believe,
a loudly dressed White man
in charcoaled face
lips painted ruby red or chalked white
showing ex-slaves as watermelon-eating
minstrel clowns, dancing jigs
of comical dialect onstage,
in books, to make audiences laugh
from their front-row seats
atop a fantasy pole of race.
Jimmy Crow tap-danced
a buck-and-wing routine
to show White folks that Black folks
would never be their equal.

FAMILY HISTORY

In July of '62, Ida Bell Wells was born.
When she was three
the Thirteenth Amendment set her free.
By the time she was eight
the Constitution was amended
two more times and made
Blacks equal to Whites under the law:
>The Thirteenth (1865)—ended slavery,
>The Fourteenth (1868)—made former slaves citizens
>of their state and the United States, and
>The Fifteenth (1870)—gave Black men the right to vote.

Ida was the first of the freed-from-slavery
generation—one foot stuck in slavery's muck
the other wiggling for a foothold
in freedom's promise.

Her mother, Elizabeth "Lizzie" Warrenton,
sold in Virginia, herded south in a slave coffle
linked by iron bars around necks
arrived in Mississippi, sold again
to Spires Boling, Holly Springs's
leading homebuilder.

Ida's father, James "Jim" Wells,
Mississippi-born and Mississippi-enslaved,
his master also being his father

the White ancestor lurking
in Ida's family tree
who apprenticed his son and slave
to Spires Boling to learn
the carpenter's craft
at Boling's house where Lizzie
was the family cook.
There, Ida was born.

1870

HUNGER

When northern White missionaries
came to teach former slaves to read and write,
Lizzie took Ida by the hand.
Together they'd learn to read the Bible
and Ida would study more.

Ida's father, proud of his daughter,
had her read newspapers to him
and his friends as they discussed
the lack of equality in Mississippi.

Ida's hunger for knowledge
soon outpaced the school's offerings.
She flashed smug frowns and pouts
when she thought the teacher
didn't respect her smarts.

CARE

Ida's mother's Bible reading
gave her daughter strong beliefs
in what was right and fair.
Her father's push for Black equality
taught Ida how to stand and demand.
Ida, age sixteen, was filled
with grit and determination
to get to the other side of slavery.
Yet no bold defiance could stop
yellow fever's rage.
Jim, Lizzie, and baby Stanley
died within days, leaving Ida
with five brothers and sisters,
one of whom, Eugenia, could not walk.

One neighbor family would take
James and George, twelve and eight,
while they learned their father's
carpenter trade; two families
would take Annie and Lily,
five and two, to help around their houses.
Eugenia, age fourteen, bedridden
and unwanted would have to go
to the poorhouse.

In full vigor and pride
Ida flashed her proud eyes
being sixteen did not matter.

She announced in a mixture
of spite and pride she would
care for her brothers and sisters.

BUTTERFLY

A way to describe the young
and innocent is to compare her
to the graceful flight of a butterfly,
but wagging tongues
sought to pin the wings
of too proud Ida
who without a thank-you,
rejected their help.

When her father was dying
Eugenia saw the nurse take money
from his pants pocket
and give it to the doctor.
Ida went looking for him.
A White doctor helping Blacks
in a small Mississippi town
was not hard to find.
Dr. Gray, a *humane* and *sympathetic* man
promised to get the money from his safe
and bring it to her later that night.

Neighborhood gossip turned "money"
and a "night" visit by a White man
into something dirty. Their imaginations
wallowed in a time when slaveowners

were like foxes in a henhouse.
Dr. Gray kept his word
protected and returned
Jim Wells's three hundred dollars.
Ida learned of the nasty tales
hinting at what she must have done
for the money, soiling her reputation
as a prim and proper butterfly.
She was double-trapped
in a gender and race cage.
>*I am quite sure that never in all my life*
>*have I suffered such a shock.*

Holly Springs
1878–1881

BIRD IN A CAGE

Ida B. Wells, free as a bird in a cage
    her wings Jim Crow-clipped
        five siblings strapped on her back
            trying to fly to the other side of slavery.
What kind of a creature am I to become?
    She shoved open the door
        knowing she wanted more
            than a life in a double-locked cage.

COUNTRY TEACHER

Though only sixteen,
Ida found a teaching job.
Each Sunday afternoon she rode a mule
six miles to a colored country school.
She spent her nights
reading
writing
and
thinking
about the creature she would become.
Back home late on Friday
she spent the hours
washing
ironing
cooking
cleaning
and
caring
until it was time on Sunday
to return to her country school.
Ida held her family together
but yearned of a life for herself.

IOLA

Ida's pride and determination
was not enough, fate and disaster
continued to rip her family apart.
Eugenia died and Ida's grandmother
who cared for the five brothers and sisters
during the week had a stroke and died.
Ida had no choice but to let
relatives take James and George
but she refused to completely surrender
to the hardships. Ida packed her sisters
Lily and Annie and headed to Memphis
for a better-paying teaching job.

While she studied for the teacher's test
Ida taught in a Tennessee country school.
Rode a train, not a mule,
to the rural colored school.
One weekend on a holiday break
she tangled with the conductor.
You know what happened next:
Ida sued, won, and lost.
Needing extra money
to pay court costs
she wrote for her church's newsletter
using the pen name "Iola."
When southern Black newspapers
reprinted her articles

she became a famous name
that wasn't hers.

Ida said she wrote in a
plain, common-sense way
on things which concerned our people.
I never used a word with two syllables
where one would serve the purpose.
I signed these articles "Iola."

Using the name "Iola"
protected her teaching job in Memphis
gave her freedom to scold
when she thought what others were doing
was not right or fair
but because of her church writings
most folks knew she was Ida.
Besides, the *o* and *l* in Iola,
if pushed together
looked like the *d* in I*d*a.

Memphis
1889

SUCCESS

Ida saved her dollars
wrote and kept teaching
and bought a third
of a money-losing newspaper—
the *Memphis Free Speech and Headlight.*

At twenty-seven, Ida B. Wells
was a teacher, newspaper publisher,
and investigative reporter.
Journalism became her passion
and with a fearless pen
she flew toward success.

Memphis
1891

SCHOOL SCANDAL

Ida taught in a crumbling building
lifted the next generation from slavery's past
with hand-me-down textbooks
marked and marred with ugly words
and pages torn out.

In Ida's view, a few teachers
fell below the behavior standards
needed if children were to rise above
slavery's mud and muck.
To raise the moral norm
she published a bombshell:
Some teachers were hired because
of relationships with important White men!

An outrageous lie, cried the school board
until a teacher's romantic affair
with a married man on the White school board
became a public nightmare,

and the teacher chose death by suicide
rather than be ostracized.

The lover denied the connection
but sent the biggest funeral
flower arrangement
the church had ever seen.
If Ida felt guilty, she did not say.
"Iola," her safety name, however,
did not protect her from being fired.

FREE SPEECH

No longer a teacher,
Ida transformed her newspaper:
bought half-ownership
shortened it to *Free Speech*
printed it on easy-to-recognize pink paper
giving status to buyers
whether they could read or not.
Some snapped up *Free Speech*
for the latest news.
Some flipped through
for a mention of their names
or of others they knew
when discovered, a blast of importance
tingled their pride.

Circulation rose from fifteen hundred
to four thousand.
A woman editor and correspondent

was a novelty.
Income rose to within ten dollars
of her teaching salary.
Male colleagues in a mix
of pride and envy
dubbed her
>   *Princess of the Press.*

March 1892

TOMMIE MOSS

Ida's friend Tommie Moss,
a mail carrier, brought news
from other parts of town,
news she turned into stories
giving readers another reason
to buy her pink paper.

In spring of '92, Ida sought
subscribers in Natchez, Mississippi.
One state away was not far enough
for the pain and tears that came:
Tommie and two friends
LYNCHED
for the unforgivable crime
of standing tall
when Jim Crow demanded
them to stoop.

THE CURVE

When Tommie asked for protection
for his grocery store
in the Black part of town
called the Curve—
where the streetcar turned around
heading back
to the White part of town—
the Memphis police claimed
the Curve wasn't in their jurisdiction.

Tommie carried mail by day,
ran a grocery store at night.
The White grocer down the street
had the Curve's only store
until Tommie set up shop
and turned his world upside down.

March 5, 1892

SHOWDOWN

A Saturday-night showdown
after a Friday-night argument:
White men swore they'd return.
Black men pledged they'd be ready.
Tommie, friends, and a few more guns waited.

When the White men arrived
Black men shot first,
wounded two or three.

Then the story changed.
Memphis police could protect Whites
in the part of town
where the streetcar turned around.
Tommie and two of his friends
were hauled to jail. Charges serious:
one White man shot—a policeman—
his wound thought fatal.
A lynch mob was expected:
no trial necessary.

A Black posse with ready guns
stood guard outside the jail
to protect their friends
from the expected rabble.
Sunday and Monday
came and went without trouble.
Tuesday morning, good news:
The policeman would survive.
The Black posse went home.

March 9, 1892
2:30 a.m.

THE LYNCHING

Masked men unlocked the jailhouse door
dragged Tommie and his friends
to a deserted part of town.
A local reporter wrote
an eyewitness account:

> Tommie begged for his life
> cried he had a wife
> a daughter
> and another baby on the way.

The killers laughed and asked
if he had a final request.
Tommie said:
Tell my people to go West—
there is no justice for them here.

The White reporter who watched
three Black men beg for their lives
wrote of their murders as if it were
a public-service event:

> *one of the most orderly*
> *of its kind ever conducted . . .*

The vengeance was sharp, swift, and sure
but administered with due regard
of the fact that people were asleep all around the jail.

IDA'S PEN

Ida returned from Mississippi,
found Tommie's store empty.
White grocery shelves bulged
with Tommie's goods.
She took out her pen
sharpened it to its finest point,
plunged it into Jim Crow's heart.

Ida wanted to know
what made the White caricature
of black-faced Jimmy Crow
change from a dancing clown
to a beast that had to be put down?

Was it a sick display of racial pride
hanging
shooting
castrating
and burning?
For victims, a message heard
at their last terrified breath
that they were lesser beings.

For Ida B. Wells,
it became a crusade
to find the reason why
Jim Crow became enraged,

extinguished Black lives
for an evening's entertainment.

REASONS

Ida wondered, did she have the courage
to write that Tommie and friends
were lynched to stop them
from competing with a White grocer
in the Black part of town?

Was she bold and brave enough
to find the reasons why lynchings
were as common as apple pie?
Could she do what was unheard
of for a woman Black or White?
  Visit lynching sites
  Interview witnesses
  Use White newspaper descriptions
  of Black lynchings
  Speak with loved ones
  Tell the victims' side of the story.
She did and concluded:
  Rape, a ghastly act, and an ugly word
  often given as a reason for Jim Crow's
  grisly act.
Cries of Black rape painted
former slaves as lusty brutes
but were these false excuses
for forbidden romances
across the color line?

TAUNT

Before leaving for a church convention
in Philadelphia and on to New York City
for vacation, Ida printed her findings
in her pink newspaper:
The South resented giving
the Afro-American his freedom,
the ballot box, and the Civil Rights Law.
She told what she'd uncovered:
Eight Negroes lynched since
the last issue of 'Free Speech' . . .

Nobody in this section of the country
believes the old threadbare lie
that Negro men rape white women.

Knowing her story would find its way
to White men's fear
of White women's romance
across the color line,
she added a taunt,
      If Southern white men
      are not careful
false charges of rape will lead
the public to a conclusion,
      very damaging
      [to] *the moral reputation of their women.*
Some Black readers found it funny,
others found it risky,

White men found it outrageous
called for a lynching.

OUTRAGE

The *Evening Scimitar*
with a White readership
reprinted Ida's editorial
and then challenged men
to avenge the insult.
Not knowing that a woman
wrote the story, the editor
directed how the writer
should be lynched:
>	*tie the wretch who utters these calumnies*
>	*to a stake at the intersection of Main and Madison Sts.,*
>	*brand him in the forehead with a hot iron and perform*
>	*upon him a surgical operation with a pair of tailor's*
>	*shears.*

Ida's business manager
made it out of Memphis
his body parts intact
but could not save their newspaper
from a mob attack.
>	*'Free Speech' was as if*
>	*it had never been*
a distraught Ida wrote from New York.

144

Since my business has been destroyed
and I am an exile from home.

October 1892

EXILE

Months later, while still in New York
Ida launched an anti-lynching crusade.
Somebody must show that
the Afro-American race
> *is more sinned against than sinning,*
> *and it seems to have fallen upon me to do so.*

She wrote a pamphlet
> *Southern Horrors:*
> *Lynch Law in All Its Phases*
gave the English-speaking world
the first inside story of Negro lynching.

Southern Horrors catalogued
nine years of White rage—
seven hundred and twenty-eight
monstrous deaths. In a third of them,
the charge was rape whether true or not:
> No attempt made to discover the truth
> no trials allowed
> executions carried out.

TELLING HER STORY ABROAD

Southern Horrors told the story
no one else dared to tell:
Lynching was a way
to keep Blacks from freedom's promise.
Frederick Douglass, in the introduction
of her pamphlet, called Ida
>   *Brave Woman!*

Ida's story was read
from Birmingham, Alabama,
to Birmingham, England.
Ten thousand copies sold,
a thousand in Memphis alone
turning a spotlight on
how little Black lives mattered.

Ida's fame grew from Memphis
to New York, Chicago,
and across the ocean.
Twice invited to Scotland and England,
she raised an international outcry
against lynching's slaughter.
A newspaper called her
>   *the nemesis of Southern lynchers.*

But White editors in the States
warned that she damaged
America's reputation.

WHITE CITY

Between trips to Great Britain
Ida was pulled to Chicago by
another story that needed to be told.
The Columbian Exposition,
a world's fair, opened its gates
to more than 27 million
who came to see what countries
from around the world
touted as their achievements.
The exhibits were displayed
in white-painted buildings
that gave the fairgrounds
its name—White City.

The United States commemorated
the four hundredth anniversary
of Christopher Columbus's arrival
with an array of exhibits
boasting of American achievements
but nothing of African Americans.
Ida came to correct this wrong.
She wrote:
The Reason Why
the Colored American Is Not
in the World's Columbian Exposition.
Ida argued the story of Black achievement
in the twenty-eight years since slavery:
would have been the greatest tribute

to the greatness and progressiveness
of American institutions
which could have been shown the world.

BLACK CLOWNS

The Reason Why did not alter
America's exhibits.
There was no interest in showcasing
Black achievements as a model
of the country's *greatness.*
The exposition's organizers
had hosted "Colored People's Day"
with truckloads of free watermelons,
showing the world America,
the country of White Cities
and Black Clowns.

Chicago, Illinois
June 27, 1895

DO YOU TAKE THIS MAN?

Ida had many suitors.
She found them too weak.
They found her too strong.
A woman who didn't blush
when writing about rape and murder
was not lady enough.

Ida wrote for the *Chicago Conservator,*
the city's oldest Black newspaper
whose publisher, Ferdinand Barnett,
a successful lawyer, was neither too weak
nor found Ida too strong
when she wrote about lynching and sex.

Ida married Ferdinand, and friends worried
how she could be married to a man
while still married to a cause?
They needn't have worried.
Ida B. Wells, reformer, journalist, wife
would not get lost
in her husband's shadow.
She attached his name to hers—
Ida B. Wells-Barnett
and confessed that being a journalist
was my first, and might be said, my only love.

Chicago
1895

THE RED RECORD

Ida's crusade against lynching
made good-hearted people aware
but did little to stop the nightmarish habit
of stringing Black bodies from trees.
Ida wrote another pamphlet
on the scourge of lynching:
The Red Record

in which she tabulated Jim Crow's
grotesque entertainments.

Readers shuddered at Ida's recounting
of the hot iron torture of Henry Smith
and his corpse burning while a crowd cheered.
It was more truth than many readers could take.

THE EXPERT

Ida traveled west and east
crusading against the national crime.
Her reception was cold
The Red Record sales low
the story too brutally told.
The White press pushed back
claimed Ida a troublemaker
who made a living by disturbing
good-hearted Americans.

John Jacks of the Missouri Press Association
sent a letter to Ida's English supporters
to topple her from her worldwide platform.
Jacks, son of a slaveowner,
and a self-proclaimed Negro expert
boasted he had
lived for years where negroes are plentiful . . .
are wholly devoid of morality . . .
the women were prostitutes.

It was Ida's time to shudder:
> *he libeled not only me, but the Negro*
> *womanhood of the country through me.*

Jim Crow not only danced and murdered
but propagandized to keep her people
from reaching the other side of slavery:
Black men were rapists
Black women prostitutes.

March 1896
Washington, D.C.

THE LINK

Frederick Douglass endorsed Ida's
investigative reports—
Southern Horrors and *The Red Record.*
They were two children from slavery.
Frederick from the middle
Ida at the end, both clawed
to get to the freedom side
of slavery and its next-of-kin
Jim Crow.

The nation's notable Negro women
met in Washington, D.C.
Trailblazing Ida shockingly arrived
with her nursing baby
three-month-old Charles.
Harriet Tubman, fearless

Underground Railroad conductor,
lifted Charlie above her head
to wild applause and completed the link—
Douglass, Tubman, to Ida B. Wells—
passing the reformer's torch
from hand to hand to hand
with the future of a new life.

Washington, D.C.
1898

MOBOCRACY

President William McKinley
appointed a Black man, Frazier B. Baker,
to the government job of postmaster
in a small South Carolina town—
a job a Black shouldn't have,
thought the White citizens of Lake City.
A mob shot up Baker's house
target-practiced on his wife
and five children as they fled
their burning home where Baker
and infant daughter Julia lay dead.

Ida went to Washington
with a committee of eight
and urged President McKinley
to use the power of the federal government
hunt down those responsible
and make lynching a federal crime.

The President, a former governor
of Ohio, had been a staunch
defender of Black lives
but was now dependent on the support
of White congressmen
whose voters had little interest
in making Black lives safe.

The government did investigate.
Indicted thirteen for the murder lynching
of postmaster Baker and his infant daughter
but an all-White jury appointed
by the state found them not guilty.

In November a mass mob murder
was carried out in Wilmington, North Carolina,
leaving hundreds of Black bodies in its wake.
President McKinley was mum
on the North Carolina massacre.
He ignored Ida's demand for a federal
crime bill against lynching.
Ida grew more determined to expose
how Jim Crow murdered her people
and how the federal government
took no interest in stopping
the heinous deeds
because White votes mattered
more than Black lives.

PAMPHLETEER

Like Thomas Paine
and Alexander Hamilton
who wrote pamphlets
in support of American independence
and the ratification of the Constitution,
Ida B. Wells was a pamphleteer
who wrote to liberate Black Americans
from Jim Crow's deadly grip.

The pamphlets flowed from her pen:
 Southern Horrors (1892)
 The Reason Why (1893)
 The Red Record (1895)
 The Lynch Law in Georgia (1899)
 Mob Rule in New Orleans (1900)
More would follow!
The outcry grew louder.
Ida B. Wells made
good-hearted Americans ashamed
of their country. Her pamphleteering
had to be stopped, even though lynchings
and mob murder continued to rise.

Boston
January 1900

NATIONAL CRIME

A new year, a new century,
the same hate-filled problem
shook Ida's pen.
She told White readers
of *The Arena* magazine:
Our country's national crime is lynching.
The new century was linked to the last
    with the inhuman butchery
infecting the country, becoming more
voracious from lynching of one to three
to mass murders of hundreds by
White mobs keeping Blacks
from reaching the other side of slavery.

Springfield, Illinois
August 14–16, 1908

A SWARM

August, the time of year
when short-horned grasshoppers
and people go crazy with summer heat.
A swarm of men, women, and children
landed near Abraham Lincoln's monument
chewed and buzzed on the news—

two Black men who had murdered and raped
were in jail.

Police heard the buzzing
hustled their prisoners to safety.
Outraged that there was no one
to snatch and string, the mob buzzed
through Black neighborhoods shouting:
>Lincoln freed you,
>now we'll show you where you belong.

Five thousand White locusts swarmed
through the Black part of town:
>two innocent men lynched
>sixteen more dead
>eighteen fires blazed
>$150,000 worth of property
>looted and destroyed
>in Abraham Lincoln's hometown.

New York City
June 1, 1909

LIST-MAKERS

Out of Springfield's ashes
a new group rose—
the National Association for the Advancement
of Colored People—
the first interracial group fighting Jim Crow.

A meeting in New York City
would name the Founding Forty
to launch the NAACP.
Confident she would be
one of the chosen,
Ida waited past midnight
but her name was not announced.
Who had fought lynching's plague longer?
She stomped from the meeting
with anger and unkind thoughts.

The list-makers explained:
wealthy White donors were needed
for the organization to thrive.
Ida's outspoken one-woman crusade
made her too controversial.
Friends pushed and squabbled
until her name was added.
Message sent:
>Ida could be a member but not a leader.
She felt blindsided
>*at the hands of the men*
>*of my own race.*
She knew the reason why:
>she was a dark-skinned woman
>more self-educated than college trained.
The new organization wanted polite
lightly colored college-bred men
to better coax dollars from
wealthy White wallets.

Cairo, Illinois
November 11, 1909

INVESTIGATION

A double lynching in southern Illinois
announced once again that Jim Crow
was evil and rampant.
To beat back the monster
all fighters were needed
but Black leaders in Chicago
thought the Cairo lynchings
were not worth the effort.
One victim White
the other a no-good Black roustabout.

Ida disagreed. A state law required
sheriffs to protect their prisoners.
Had the sheriff obeyed the law?
If enforced, it could prevent other lynchings.
Ida went to Cairo to find out
because no one else would.

Willy "Froggie" James was hanged,
shot, burnt, and beheaded
as 10,000 cheered and sliced
poor Willy's charred remains for souvenirs.
The bloodlust continued to rage:
The mob dragged Henry Salzner
from his cell, strung him from a telegraph pole
punctured his pale corpse with pistol bullets
and shotgun pellets.

IDA'S QUESTION

Had the sheriff done all he could?
Ida visited the killing sites
>   read newspaper accounts
>   held a mass meeting
>   caught the night train
>   to Springfield the state capital
>   and shared her findings with the governor.

Had the sheriff done all he could?
Ida proved he had not!
The governor deliberated, then agreed.
The sheriff lost his job and other sheriffs
started paying attention to the law.

Ida returned to Chicago
to praise from some
but envy from those unwilling
to protest the lynching of a White murderer
and a no-good Black roustabout.
One newspaper stung the prestigious Black leaders:
if we only had a few men with the backbone
>   *of Mrs. [Ida] Barnett, lynching would soon come to a halt.*

Washington, D.C.
March 3, 1913

THE VOTE

A suffrage march on the eve
of President Wilson's inauguration
spotlighted women's struggle
to have a say in how the country
should behave.
Ida, representing her
Alpha Suffrage Club, was asked
to step aside, not to march
with Illinois White suffragists.
If she wanted to march
she should find a Black group
at the back of the line.

On the day of the march
five thousand women stepped through
the jeering crowds of heckling men.
Ida was not there.
Was she on a train home
or in the way-back where she belonged?
A few blocks later
smiles turned to frowns:
Ida pushed through the jeering men,
joined arm in arm with two White friends.
The trio led the Illinois suffragists
marching for women's rights and the
      VOTE!

FAIR OR FOUL

In the nation's capital, fireworks burst
Confederate flags flapped
Virginia-born Woodrow Wilson
was President of the United States.
Wilson's views on race years before
had made Jim Crow's chalked white lips grin
      White men could use *fair means or foul*
      to keep *ignorant negroes* in their place.

Ida went to Washington with a committee of seven
to plead with President Woodrow Wilson
to stop dismissing Blacks from their federal jobs.

She saw she was mistaken to hope
the meeting would lead the President
to change.
Refusing to sit with his Negro guests
he stood for thirty-five minutes
and saw no reason why Blacks
needed federal protection against lynching.
It was best left to the states to prosecute
if they thought a crime had been committed.
After the meeting he continued
to segregate government buildings
with Whites-only cafeterias and toilets.

WHAT ABOUT ME?

World War I went into full swing.
As in the Civil War, Black soldiers
weren't wanted until there was no other choice.
The government kept them in segregated regiments
but the soldiers could not keep from asking:
If I fight to save democracy
what about me?

No matter how many died
in trenches across the sea
Black soldiers would die at home
for asking: What about me?

East St. Louis, on the Illinois side
of the Mississippi River, answered
with a three-day killing spree—
a white-hot riot with more Black bodies
than the government would acknowledge.

As a good reporter does,
Ida took the train to find the reasons why.
The conductor warned: not a place to be.
Undaunted, Ida walked into the downtown area.
The city hall janitor, the only Black person
still in town, warned:
East St. Louis not a safe place to be.

EAST ST. LOUIS MASSACRE

She found survivors hiding outside of town
and wrote their horrific tales
of how the State National Guard
blocked the bridge across the river
leaving no escape from the white-hot mob.
Some victims attempted to swim the Mississippi
only to be shot, stoned, or drowned.

By the thousands, Blacks had moved to East St. Louie
pushed out of the South by Jim Crow,
pulled to the North by better-paying jobs.
Dreaming, like any immigrant
forced to flee their homeland,
of a better life ahead.
Their arrival and competition
hinted of troubles.
Black dentist LeRoy Bundy feared
what was coming,
appealed to the governor for protection.
Trouble was a-brewing,
race blood in the air.

The State Guard arrived
but didn't stop a carload of Whites
shooting up Black homes.
Dr. Bundy and his crew shot back.
This is where the story became the same:
two policemen reported slain.

Ida published her findings
with a title that set feelings frying:
> The East St. Louis Massacre:
> The Greatest Outrage of the Century.

The pamphlet raised funds
for Dr. Bundy's defense
and saved him from the electric chair.
Ida's go-alone crusade
increased her reputation
though powerful Black men in Chicago
believed her influence too strong,
denounced her as a radical, someone
Whites should be leery of.

July 27, 1919

CHICAGO

Ida fifty-seven years into life
twenty-four years in the Windy City
a long way from a mule-riding teacher
or mulatto passenger tossed from a train
yet still in the gender cage, unable to vote,
race still a heavy stone tied to her ankles.

The upside-down world had traveled north,
hit a White wall as solid as the South's.
Blacks from Tennessee, Mississippi, Arkansas
Alabama, and Georgia had flooded Chicago
and Midwestern cities with Black refugees.
Chicago turned darker between 1909 and 1920

from 44,000 to 110,000;
Chicago turned whiter as European immigrants
arrived to work in packing houses alongside Blacks
slaughtering cows, pigs, and sheep
for the nation's dinner tables.
Blacks and Whites wrestled
for a seat at the American table.
On a hot July Sunday
Ida sat at home in Chicago
away from the city's hate
that inflamed the attack on
seventeen-year-old Eugene Williams
but she learned of it soon enough:
It was Memphis and Tommie Moss
all over again.

COLOR LINE

Eugene Williams on his swimming raft
in Lake Michigan
between 26th and 29th Street beaches
floated across an imaginary color line
keeping Whites and Blacks apart.
Eugene and three friends
cold-splashed on a steaming day
until rocks hit their raft
a cascade of swishes and thumps
until one hit Eugene's head
turning the color line blood red.
Hours later rescuers found his body.

Chicago police rules stopped
Black cops from arresting Whites.
When both a White and a Black cop
rushed to the scene
the Black cop couldn't
the White cop wouldn't
arrest the White man who "accidentally"
drowned the colored boy with a rock.
A Black man protested.
The White cop taught him a civics lesson:
arrest the protester, set the rock-thrower free.

Chicago exploded in a rage,
fires and killings fed by wild rumors, false reports.
White gangs had the urge to kill
in the name of race,
drove speeding cars through the Black part of town
shooting into dark homes that fired back.
One car hit, a man inside shot
likely to die, reportedly, a cop.
The riot took a tragic turn:
seventeen days of rioting
38 dead and 537 wounded.

The federal government investigated.
The GID—General Intelligence Division
later renamed the FBI—was led
by J. Edgar Hoover.
He listed the troublemakers
who'd caused bad race relations
and made the race riot inevitable.
At the top of the list was Ida B. Wells

*considered by the black population of Chicago
to be some kind of superwoman.*

Paris, France
January 1919–1920

PEACE CONFERENCE

World War I came to an end
peace settled over Europe
guns fell silent.
A peace conference convened in France
with the hope that wars were forever over.
Ida planned to go and argue
that until America stopped
lynching its citizens
world peace was not possible.
The government thought
it better for Ida to stay home
and denied her a passport
so she wouldn't shame America
at the world peace conference.

Elaine, Arkansas
September 30–October 1919

RED SUMMER

The poet James Weldon Johnson
called the summer of 1919
Red Summer for its mob murder lynchings.
The summer of hate
burned into autumn, blazing
from Chicago to a small Arkansas
cotton town where twelve men
waited on Death Row
for demanding the going market price
for their cotton crop.

More than two hundred Black
children, women, and men were dead
in a two-day attack by Whites
from three states.
History called it a race riot not a massacre
as if the sharecroppers
had burned their own bodies
in the church where their union
met the last Tuesday of September.
The official report claimed
it was a meeting of conspirators
who planned to massacre Whites.
Two White men were shot—it's not clear
whether friendly fire or Black defense.
Seventy-nine Blacks were convicted
of conspiracy and sentenced to life in prison.

Twelve received the death penalty
after an eight-minute deliberation
by an all-White jury.

January 1920

THE TRUTH

Ida wrote the governor of Arkansas:
Without a new and fair trial
she would use her pen to persuade
Blacks to leave his state
robbing it of its farmworkers.
The governor listened.
Without Black workers the cotton crop
would not get picked.
A new trial was called.

Then Ida took a train to Arkansas
her first trip south since
she was run out of Memphis
thirty years before.
Pretending to be a relative
she met with the prisoners
and listened to their stories
of how union members and families
were murdered, and while they were
in jail their families were robbed
of their cotton, livestock, farm equipment,
clothes, and furniture.
Ida wrote another pamphlet laying bare

the lie as only she could:
There'd been no threat to murder Whites,
rather a scheme instead to stop the union
from demanding the same price
for their cotton that White farmers received.

Though some in Chicago
thought Ida's day had passed,
the grandmotherly crusader
sold her *Arkansas Race Riot* pamphlet
and raised money for the defense
of the twelve on death row.

Nashville, Tennessee
May 18, 1920

MEMORY

Ida, hundreds of miles away,
might have heard the shouts
from the state that chased her away
those many years ago—Tennessee.
Ratifying a woman's right to vote
corrected the Constitution
the nineteenth time.
A bittersweet celebration
twirled in Ida B. Wells's mind.
She had the vote and three Tennessee ghosts:
Tommie Moss and his friends,
gunshot lynched in Memphis
so many years ago,

lacked a federal law to correct
future murder lynching.

Washington, D.C.
January 1922

THE CONSTITUTION

Ida B. Wells, sixty years old,
began to hope. A bill to make
lynch murder a federal crime
moved through Congress.

The Fourteenth correction
to the Constitution ratified but not enforced
for fifty-eight years—
> *nor shall any state deprive any person*
> *of life, liberty, or property, without due*
> *process of law; nor deny to any person*
> *within its jurisdiction the equal protection of the laws.*
The 14th Amendment might now be enforced:
> no executions without a trial.
President Wilson nearly dead and gone.
President Harding said Congress
> *ought to wipe the stain of barbaric lynching*
> *from the banners of a free and orderly*
> *representative democracy.*

Five hundred Blacks demonstrated
in front of the White House
urged the nation to make

Ida's dream come true.
No more lynching!
The party of Abraham Lincoln
held the majority
in the House and Senate.
Ida had reasons to hope.
A new law for her homeland,
an anti-lynching bill!
It passed the House of Representatives.
The Senate Judiciary Committee
gave it a push.
Ida had reasons to smile
until once again her people
were betrayed:
Southern White votes mattered more
than Black lives.
The anti-lynching bill never made it
to the Senate floor.

NEGRO AGITATOR

Ida B. Wells grew older and cringed
at how little had changed.
She needed to keep agitating.
Two decades into
the twentieth century
twelve hundred lynched
by "persons unknown."
Senators had defeated
two hundred anti-lynching bills
claiming it was up to states to prosecute.

Congressmen from Georgia and Mississippi
failed to mention the five hundred
lynchings in their states and no arrests
of "persons unknown."

Chicago
1927

AMONG THE LIVING

Rewards come in small packages.
A stranger, his face
Ida couldn't place
but something familiar
came clear when he
explained how she'd saved
him from despair as he waited
on death row in the Arkansas penitentiary
after an eight-minute trial
found him guilty of murder
for defending himself
and wanting fair market price
for his cotton crop.

Ida had visited him
and the other eleven
in their Arkansas cells.
Urged them to stop singing
and praying about heaven.
Focus on staying alive
and getting a new trial

as she was doing because
she knew they were innocent.

Their execution delayed,
their cases went all the way
to the Supreme Court
and they were freed.
The visitor stood in her Chicago
living room grateful to Ida
for keeping him among the living.

Chicago
March 25, 1931

ETERNAL VIGILANCE

Petals dropped from the roses
near her bed.
Swirls of sugar clouds
dotted the afternoon sky.
Ida Bell Wells drifted
in and out of coma sleep,
each cloud floating a memory:
> Saw a young teacher in a Mississippi country school
>> five brothers and sisters awaiting her return.
> Saw a proud woman manhandled from the Ladies' Car
>> and a court that clipped her wings.
> Saw a fearless journalist expose the hate-filled national crime
>> that kept Black lives in Jim Crow terror.

Saw Presidents and Congress
        unwilling to make lynching a federal crime.
Saw what America needed:
        To keep asking the reason why.

MA

RTIN LUTHER KING JR.

1929-1968

This Lie Will Not Live

How long? Not long, because no lie can live forever.

—Martin Luther King Jr.

Atlanta, Georgia
1931

PASSING THE SWORD

Ida B. Wells, her pen a sword,
slashed at the horrors stalking
her people as they crossed the bridge
between the Civil War and civil rights.

Seven hundred miles south
two-year-old Martin Luther King Jr.
waited to pick up Ida's sword
and lead an army to the mountaintop.

IN THE BEGINNING

A NORDIC MYTH

A tale of deceit intoxicated
We the people
in a dizzying untruth:
A story written on a hidden stone
in a faraway land
told how the gods of old
lumped humankind
into groups called "races"
with color-coded winners and losers.

Drunk on this heady sham
people in slavery times
bought, sold, raped, and killed
those they color-coded as less.

After the Civil War
the defeated and the victorious
held fast to the ancient untruth
anointed themselves the superior clan
refused to obey
new Constitutional Amendments
Thirteen, Fourteen, and Fifteen
that gave the once-enslaved the right
to be free, equal, and live.
We will call the clan, Guardians of the Lie.

COLOR CODES

This Lie assigned wisdom to the owl
dumbness to the turkey
criminality to the darkness of human skin
moral weakness to the texture of hair
intelligence to the length
of the back of the foot.
Even now, their young inhale
this addictive untruth
like secondhand smoke
believing Asians are better at math
Blacks at basketball
Latinos at soccer
and Whites in all things that matter.

JUNIOR KING

There was once a dark son of a King
not of royalty born
but of slavery and sharecrop misery.
Daddy King named his son in honor
of the German protest preacher
from centuries before—
Martin Luther.
He gave his son the fiery voice
of a prophet and armed him
with the gospel and the law—
the Bible and Constitution—

and set him on a prophet warrior's quest
to become America's protest preacher
and convert the Guardians
from their deadly Lie.

This is the story of how the dark son
Martin Luther King Jr.
battled the Lie that marked winners
and losers by the texture of hair
or the length of a heel.
This is the story of how
America's protest preacher
converted millions of Guardians
from their intoxicating Lie
and their murderous ways.

BOOK ONE
1934–1944

MARTIN

Dinner for six in a warm Black home.
At the head of the table
Daddy King saw something amiss:
five-year-old Martin's distress.
His older sister knew why,
his baby brother, too young to care.
Mother and grandmother sensed
their little boy's pain, but waited for Daddy King
to ask Martin to explain.

His best friend since three
had reached the age
when he could no longer play.
One school for Blacks, another for Whites
was the law.
The friend's father, local grocer,
would not let his son
betray the Guardians' way
and have a friend outside the color lane.
Daddy King spoke of forgiveness
quoted the Bible:
Love your enemies,
do good to them which hate you.

Young Martin let his peas turn cold.
His daddy's idea too odd and old:
Forgive the man who took his friend away?

Atlanta, Georgia
1941

GUILT

Having preachers
for a daddy, granddaddy, and great-granddaddy
made many things a sin:
listening to music that wasn't churchy
dreaming of girls and their Hollywood looks.
Perhaps his guilt came from being twelve
or from scary bedtime prayers:
If I should die before I wake,
I pray the Lord, my soul to take.
One Sunday afternoon
Martin sneaked off to a parade.
High-stepping musicians
kept his head in beat
with unholy drums and boastful tubas.
Marching swirling girls
their shimmering brown legs
made his thoughts run wild.

A friend's tap on the shoulder
spun untamed glee into guilt.

Martin's grandmother slumped dead at church
where he should have been.
He raced home and Grandmother
was not there to tell him it was okay.
Believing he was to blame
Martin jumped from a second-floor window—
cuts and bruises received, but heaven not reached.
His flight too low for his soul to take.

Dublin, Georgia
May 1944

MASTER ORATOR

Martin saw the joy on his mother's face
when a visiting minister peppered his sermon
with words his preacher daddy did not use.
Martin promised to make her proud one day
with words his daddy could not use.

At fifteen, he'd mastered
such words and more.
At the Black Elks' Orator Festival
in Dublin, Georgia, Martin delivered
"The Negro and the Constitution."
His sentences pulsed in lyrical waves
that made the dictionary jealous.

BUS RIDE

On the ride back to Atlanta
in the colored section of the bus
Martin basked in his oratory skills.
He'd told how thirteen million
Black Americans were restricted
in where they could eat and sleep
work and learn.

At the first stop, more Whites boarded.
Martin knew he was about to take a test
he would fail.
The White section was full
the colored section too.
His teacher told him to stand.
The bus driver commanded:
Blacks stand! Whites sit!
Martin searched for an answer from his speech
but its truth went missing.
Defy his teacher, defy the driver
and be left on the highway?
Martin's courage wilted.
He did as the Guardians' law demanded
stood for ninety miles
in an angry puddle of shame.

Simsbury, Connecticut
Summer 1944

SWEAT AND FUN

The country at war
soldiers on battlefields around the world
Connecticut tobacco farms empty of hands.
Martin, fifteen, first time away from home
first time north, worked tobacco
to earn college funds
in a summer of sweat and fun.

On Saturdays, he and the other Black college boys
sipped Dr Peppers at the local drugstore
ate in restaurants they could afford.
No rules or customs kept them at bay.
The rest of the week
Martin and his exhausted friends
laughed themselves to sleep
with exaggerated stories of sports and girls.

TRAIN RIDE

The summer of sweat and fun over
tobacco leaves tied and stored
Martin headed home
rode from Hartford to D.C.
in an integrated train
then rode in a Jim Crow–segregated train

for all points south.
Hungry and without a shoebox
of Mama King's fried chicken
he went to the dining car
took a seat at a white linen table
with its single red carnation.
The Black waiter shook his head.
The White steward in a swirl
of disdain moved
Martin behind a gray curtain.
Eating in the same space as Whites
was against the Guardians' law.

A PLEDGE

On the long bus ride after his
"Negro and the Constitution" speech
Martin had known in his mind
where he wanted his body to be.
Returning home on a Jim Crow train
the same shame of being coded by color.

Martin Luther King Jr., age fifteen,
left for college; at nineteen
became a minister
but was unsure of how to challenge
the addictive untruth that kept him
behind a curtain of hate.

BOOK TWO
1944–1967

GOLD MEDALS

A decade of schooling placed
gold medals of learning
around Martin's neck.
Transformed him into Dr. King
a man in a hurry to be more than
a Georgia country preacher.

A nut-brown man in a white peasant cloth
changed Martin more than any college degree:
Mohandas Gandhi, an Indian lawyer
whose nonviolent protests
brought Great Britain's colonial rule
and plunder of India to its knees.
Martin studied Gandhi's teachings
sought a way to change
the Guardian plunder
of American Blacks
with the restrictions at voting booths
control over where they could work,
live, go to school, eat, and be buried.
Black lives were no longer enslaved
but shackled by slavery's next of kin:
Jim Crow segregation.
Gandhi showed Martin another way
to love those who hate you.

HEART BREAKER

On his educational speedway
Martin left broken hearts
from Georgia to Pennsylvania.
He and his friends anointed themselves
the Wreckers for conquest
of many loves enjoyed
before moving to another.
But in Boston, Cupid chuckled,
hit him with the arrow
that put the wrecking days on hold.

An Atlanta friend knew an "Alabama girl"
a student at a celebrated Boston music school.
Martin called Coretta Scott
sight unseen, swore his affection,
said every Napoleon had his Waterloo—
she had captured him before they even met.
Smart, attractive Coretta, two years older
two years wiser than her outlandish caller
with his comic book lines.

The same Atlanta friend had told Coretta
about Martin, how his daddy,
Atlanta's highest-paid Black preacher,
was a civil rights leader.

Told her Martin was certain to climb high.
His preaching style and many degrees
made him a star on the rise.

CUPID

Coretta agreed to take a look.
First date, she didn't like his age
or brash ways but remained intrigued.
More dates: thought him serious, but fun;
intense about religion, but loved to dance;
somber, but a fan of opera;
earnest about changing the world.
Brash though, too brash, way too fast.

He told her she had the beauty and brains
he wanted in a wife, words from a man
in a hurry to be somebody.
Coretta, unsure she wanted
to be his somebody,
wanted to slow it down, determined
to be her own somebody.

Martin asked his sister to sing his praises
asked Coretta's sister to join the refrain.
At last, he won his love's heart.

Sixteen months after they met,
an Alabama wedding.
Daddy King blessed Martin and Coretta

to be faithful for all their living days.
No Honeymoon Inn could be found.
Not a hotel for Blacks within a hundred miles.
A funeral home had to do.

Montgomery, Alabama
1954

MONTGOMERY

Jim Crow segregation in the North
floated like a virus, difficult to discern,
deadly to catch.
In the south, segregation easier to see
danced on the end of a rope.
After years in Boston, Martin and Coretta
moved South.
A church in Montgomery needed a minister.
Martin needed a congregation.
The church was built on the grounds
of an old slave market
near the Alabama state capitol
with its Confederate and American flags
swaying in a twisted history—
one honoring the nation
the other applauding the rebels
who tried to destroy it.

HOW TO RIDE A BUS

Martin and Coretta's arrival
made church elders proud.
With baby Yolanda on the way
Black Montgomery beamed
their young minister and his
thumbtack-sharp wife
birthing a better tomorrow.
But if they caught a bus
they had to enter by the front door,
pay their dime, step off,
reenter through the back door,
sit in the colored section.
When the section filled
they could sit in "no man's land"
between the White and colored sections
until the White section was full
and the driver commanded:
Blacks stand! Whites sit!

Money, Mississippi
August 24, 1955

GORE

If there was any doubt
that Martin and Coretta had returned
to Jim Crow South,
Mississippi, one state to the west
startled them awake.

The Guardians struck a kid
who didn't know the trouble he was in.
Emmett Till, recently turned fourteen,
from Chicago and a summer visitor,
bought candy at the country store.
Carolyn Bryant, the White storeowner's wife,
testified
This nigger man came into the store.
He caught my hand . . . and asked,
How about a date, baby?
Carolyn claimed Emmett did more.
Decades later, on her deathbed
she confessed she'd made up
most of the story.
But on an August night in '55
Carolyn's husband and his half brother
tortured and murdered Emmett Till
in a festival of gore.

November 1955

VISITING SPEAKER

Dr. T. R. M. Howard
a civil rights leader
spoke at Martin's Dexter Baptist Church
told the details of Emmett's murder.
In the congregation sat Rosa Parks.
Four days later she sparked the
civil rights movement.

BOYCOTT

On a December day, Rosa Parks
paid her dime the same as the White
who wanted her seat.
She refused, no matter how loud
the driver growled.
Rosa Parks, perhaps thinking
of Emmett's mother,
would take it no more.
Hauled to jail, charged a ten-dollar fine
for breaking the law that must be obeyed.

In protest of Rosa's arrest
Martin asked Black Montgomery
to walk, not ride, in a one-day boycott
to show that without Black riders
the city would lose a lot of dimes.
Other ministers joined.
Ralph Abernathy of First Baptist,
Montgomery's largest Black church,
saw in Martin a new kind of leader
who would use the Bible
and the Constitution to fight Jim Crow's laws.
Ralph became Martin's trusted advisor
and forever friend.

BLACK DIMES

On a Monday morning, the boycott began.
Buses rolled through the Black part of town
with empty seats. Sidewalks crowded
with old and young walking for sister Rosa
and the dignity of their daily lives.
The one-day boycott succeeded.
Then came the question:
Continue the boycott until
the city ended segregated seating?
Or start riding and hope the city
would desegregate?
Martin convinced Black Montgomery
to do what Mohandas Gandhi would have done.
Keep walking!
Martin and his committee
proposed a modest plan:
Blacks enter the front door
pay their dime
go straight to the back
no reboarding required.
Whites in the first four rows
Blacks in the back rows
but the middle section—
first come, first served.
Blacks did not have to give up their seats.
Whites were to stand when the front
and middle section were full.
Drivers would be courteous to all
and Black drivers would cover routes
in Black neighborhoods.

LONG ANSWER

The plan rejected
violated Jim Crow's decree
as necessary as the wind that swayed
two flags in their twisted history.

The boycott continued.
Folks walked until their soles
were scraped paper-thin.
Rosa Parks arrested,
which the faithful protested.
Black ministers jailed
and Black Montgomery walked
and carpooled for six months.

Martin and Coretta received
threatening calls, but loyal folks
rode and walked any way they could.
Eight months, and the boycott continued.
Coretta encouraged the discouraged.
Martin fortified the weary.
The boycott at eleven months
did not stop when Martin went to jail.

SUCCESS

Black Montgomery sued.
A federal district court agreed
the bus law was unfair and wrong.
The city appealed, argued without shame
that Blacks were color-coded as lesser
human beings.
The boycott continued.
Folks walking, carpooling
until the Supreme Court declared
Blacks could sit in an empty bus seat!

Martin had done the impossible.
Led a 381-day boycott
wiped away a Jim Crow law—
his first steps toward becoming
America's protest preacher.

RESPONSE

You can't poke a beehive
and not get stung.
The Guardians had held power
for three centuries—
someone had to get stung.
Martin's house BOMBED.
Martin's friend Ralph Abernathy's
house BOMBED.

The house of White ally
Rev. Robert Graetz BOMBED.
And five Black churches BOMBED.

Martin's courage was tested.
He bought a gun.
Ralph chastised his friend
who had promised to love the enemy
no matter how hateful.
Martin gave up the gun
but was left to wonder:
If the Guardians were this vicious
over empty bus seats,
what would they do
when he demanded more?

Atlanta, Georgia
January 1959

NEXT

Montgomery a first victory
but more battles had to be waged
against the monster of racial arrogance
that stigmatized and dehumanized
with race-based bus seats, jobs, and schools.

Martin founded the Southern Christian
Leadership Conference (SCLC),
moved to Atlanta and became co-pastor
of Daddy King's church, Ebenezer Baptist.
Two demanding jobs—for the man in a hurry.

Birmingham, Alabama
1963

MAGIC OR TRAGIC

Whites called Birmingham the Magic City
for their many good jobs.
Blacks called it Tragic City
for its poor-paying jobs
and bomb-enforced segregation.
A local leader invited Martin
to help integrate the color-coded
lunch counters, bathrooms,
department stores, and drinking fountains

that made the city Magic for Whites
and Tragic for Blacks.

Birmingham Blacks had reasons to fear
trying to change how they were constrained.
The poor saw no reason to turn the other cheek.
The slightly better off couldn't risk their jobs.
The few better off had too much to lose
and too little to gain,
but they all had a greater fear:
The chief Guardian had a nickname
as scary as the nightstick he carried:
The Bull.
Theophilus Eugene "Bull" Connor,
in charge of the police and fire departments,
had a double-fisted power to keep the city
Tragic and Magic.

EASTER SHOPPING

Martin launched what he called
Plan C, for CONFRONTATION.
Less a plan, more a trap
to provoke hot-tempered Bull:
      expose Birmingham's color-coded laws
      attract the press because
      nonviolent protest and confrontation
      with the Bull would make the news.
Front-page coverage would draw more folks
from the Tragic City side of Birmingham
to protest the Jim Crow laws.

But the Bull didn't charge.
After days, the press lost interest.
Nothing to report other than a few
churchgoing Negroes singing
"*We Shall Overcome.*"
To keep the press in place
Martin decided to be the red flag
and make the mad Bull charge.
Instead of staying out of the battle zone
to better direct the battle,
Martin would lead the marchers.

THE BULL

Martin Luther King Jr.
was a tempting target:
the Bull's officers pounced
yanked Martin by the back of his pants
shoved him into one police van
and Ralph into another.
Photographers caught the arrest
but couldn't capture how Martin felt.
He was not allowed to call Coretta
or a lawyer.
He spent Good Friday in a cell
fearing this was where his life
would end and found no comfort
in the resurrection story.

Tuesday
April 16, 1963

A LETTER

While Martin sat for nine days
in the stench of an Alabama cell
eight White religious leaders
published a letter that ran
in many Alabama newspapers
calling Martin's effort to integrate
unwise and untimely.
Martin responded with a letter
smuggled from jail.

He chastised the city's religious leaders
for ignoring their spiritual teachings
while the Guardians violated
the country's principles
of liberty and justice.
Blacks' demands for integration
were long overdue.

May 2, 1963

YOUNG CRUSADERS

Martin was out of jail.
His *Letter from Birmingham City Jail*
drew no response; the campaign
to integrate downtown stores
was on the verge of failure.
In his absence, Plan C abandoned
another plan launched.
A new army, a corps
of teenage crusaders,
younger than sixteen
braver than their parents,
marched to the front
wrapped their future in freedom.

They were an army
Martin didn't want to use
but gave his consent
to send teenagers into the streets
rather than lose the battle of Birmingham.

Word of the new plan, D-Day,
put school principals on alert
classrooms doors locked
fence gates chained in case students
decided to join the crusade.
Teachers knew of the plan
but dared not risk their jobs.
They turned their backs
claimed they didn't see
their scholars climb out
classroom windows
and over padlocked fences.

While Martin worried
in his makeshift office
at the Gaston Motel
the teenage crusaders headed
to the Sixteenth Street Baptist Church
and solemnly swore to love their enemies.
By the end of D-Day
they had kept their oath.
The Bull kept his as well.
He force-marched hundreds
of young protesters to the fairgrounds
and locked them in stockyard pens.

WATER BLAST

The next day, a Double D-Day,
Martin directed this second wave.
More kids went out windows and over fences.
A few adults joined the flow.
An ebony tsunami surged
to the Sixteenth Street Baptist Church
and pledged an oath of nonviolence.
The young crusaders flooded
the city's business section,
swamping streets, department stores,
public libraries as if they had the right
to spend money or read a library book
their parents' tax dollars had bought.

It was too much for the Bull:
"Disperse or you're going to get wet!"
A water blast launched with bazooka force
took down the young army,
slammed them against walls.
One somersaulted end-over-end
until she flattened on the sidewalk.
The Bull with his overheating heart
called for the dogs, the K-9 teams'
German shepherds, trained Guardian-mean
to snarl, bite, and rip.
Martin in his hotel office room
cringed and prayed when he heard
how his young army were knocked

off their feet and canine terrorized.
Yet he held to his belief that it showed
how the Guardians fought
to keep their hateful ways.

Hands-over-your-mouth images
flashed across television screens:
Black children plastered against walls
cornered by snapping dogs.
An elderly woman on the ground beaten
by five of the Bull's henchmen
a knee pressed on her throat.
Martin was right. It showed the world
what it took to keep the Lie in place.

May 11–12, 1963

BOMBINGHAM

Black adults, seeing the courage
of their young, had joined the continuing
marches and demonstrations.
Because of protests in the business section
no shopping could be done.
Business leaders weighed the loss
of sales against the privilege
of segregation, discovered Jim Crow
was too expensive.
They agreed to integrated dressing rooms,
lunch counters, and restrooms.
A few agreed to hire Black clerks.

Martin Luther King Jr. again proved
that even when Guardian mobs attacked,
the protesters held to their
nonviolence creed.

Martin halted the demonstrations.
Some Whites were pleased.
Others wanted revenge,
driven to a blood-rage frenzy
by Martin *Lucifer* King.
Someone had to pay.
They turned to their weapon of choice,
dynamite.
The house of Martin's younger brother
now a Birmingham minister
BOMBED.
No deaths, no arrests.
The Gaston Motel where Martin worked
and stayed
BOMBED.
No deaths, no arrests, but a message sent:
Beware!

THE FBI

Martin turned Birmingham upside down
knocked the Bull back.
But an old opponent to Black civil rights
stepped from the shadows:
J. Edgar Hoover, director of the FBI,
firm believer in the intoxicating Lie
that winners and losers were color-coded.
As a young federal agent years earlier
he'd falsely named Ida B. Wells
the cause of the 1919 Chicago Riots.
The FBI had kept tabs on Martin
since the Montgomery Bus Strike.
Hoover, now older, fatter, and more
powerful, was determined to make
Martin Luther King Jr. a loser.

Washington, D.C.
June 11, 1963

GOSPEL AND LAW

Pictures from Birmingham showed the world
America's gap between what was professed
and what was.
President John F. Kennedy joined the fray,
spoke against the violence.
On television he explained
why he was asking Congress

to pass a Civil Rights Bill.
The President called on gospel and law:
We are confronted primarily with a moral issue.
It is as old as the scriptures and is as clear as the
American Constitution.
Almost two centuries after Thomas Jefferson
declared that all are created equal
President Kennedy announced
a new law was needed
for an American
of color to receive equal service.

Washington, D.C.
August 27, 1963

WARNING

Martin, nerves jangled in D.C.,
knew Birmingham was a success
yet unnerved he had agreed
to let kids, a few under ten, risk their lives
for the right to sit at a lunch counter.
Rattled more by lingering fears
from an earlier conversation with
President Kennedy in the Rose Garden:
The President had warned
the FBI claimed they had proof
two of Martin's advisors were agents
of a foreign government—communists.
If the FBI went public with this information
they would paint Martin as a communist dupe

and defeat the Civil Rights Bill.
The President urged King to get rid of them.

Kennedy whispered of a scandal
raging in Britain: A love affair
between the Secretary of War
and a Russian spy.
If Martin was caught in such a scandal
his moral leadership would be gone
and he would not recover.
Martin was double warned.
No Communists in his organization,
and his personal behavior,
must be scandal free.

Evening
August 27, 1963

TWENTY YEARS

Martin tamped down his spinning
troubling thoughts.
He had a speech to give.
Thought of a dream he wanted to make real
a someday when content of character
not skin color would be a balm
for the country's racial pain
and his growing anxieties.
His thoughts were pulled back
to his Black Elks speech

"The Negro and the Constitution"
and his distress ramped up
when he realized
how little had changed in twenty years.

August 28, 1963

THE GATHERING

Quarter of a million people
marched on Washington,
gathered at the Lincoln Memorial
under Abraham Lincoln's melancholic gaze.
They came because the freedom
Lincoln proclaimed was still on its way.
They would pressure Congress
to pass the Civil Rights Bill
and stop the many ways the country
kept Blacks in color-coded chokeholds.

Afternoon
August 28, 1963

THE SPEECH

Martin was the next-to-last speaker.
The crowd was tired and restless
but song after song relieved the heat
and the sameness of speaker after speaker.
Then Martin took the stage and showed

he was the voice of the civil rights movement.
He spoke a prayer of hope:
I have a dream . . .

Martin Luther King Jr.
on that sweat-soaked afternoon
pulled ideas from history and reshaped
them into a future. Now was the time
to make real the Declaration of Independence
make real the Constitution's freedom amendments
make real a new Civil Rights Bill.
Now was the time
to rid the country of noxious laws and customs
that addicted America's soul
kept Blacks locked in poverty.
He told of a day
when America would be safer for Black Americans
when Guardians would give up their Lie
when the truth that humans were not color-coded
into winners and losers would triumph.

Martin Luther King Jr. dreamed
of a day that had not come
but when he finished speaking
the roar of thousands and thousands
proved that someday his dream would be true.

NIGHTMARE

Hundreds of thousands buoyed Martin
and cheered the story of his dream
but in Birmingham, the Guardians of the Lie
thought his dream a nightmare.

On a bright autumn morning
"The Love That Forgives"
was the Sunday school lesson at
Sixteenth Street Baptist,
the church where hundreds of children
had pledged to be nonviolent before marching
into the Bull's power hose and dogs.
After Sunday school, four girls stood
at a washroom mirror making sure
no hair was out of place and ribbons
were tied pretty and tight.
Perhaps their serious minds
remembered the morning's lesson:
how to forgive someone who did you wrong.

NIGHTMARE CONTINUES

Before the last ribbon was tied,
a BOMB—
nineteen sticks of dynamite—
murdered
Addie Mae Collins (fourteen)
Carol Denise McNair (eleven)
Carole Rosamond Robertson (fourteen)
Cynthia D. Morris Wesley (fourteen)
They did not live to forgive the Guardians,
who'd boasted:
You just wait until after Sunday morning
and they will beg us to segregate.

Unsatisfied with the carnage of four,
outrage and killings continued:
Johnny Brown Robinson (sixteen)—shot in the back
for running from the police
after throwing a rock.
Virgil Ware (thirteen)—riding on the back
of his brother's bicycle, gunned down
by two Eagle Scouts after a Guardians rally.

Martin Luther King Jr. returned
to Tragic City burdened by six more
Black bodies swept away in a river of hatred.
To console grieving parents
and a furious community
he struggled to hold on
to his belief that love could conquer.

ASSASSINS

The year of hate not over.
John F. Kennedy pushed
a Civil Rights Bill to end
segregation in public places.
On the Friday before Thanksgiving
the President was shot as he rode
in an open-air limousine.

Kennedy's murder startled Martin.
If the most protected person in the world
could be assassinated, the least protected
would never be safe.
With profound and troubled weariness
Martin warned Coretta:
This could happen to me.
America's protest preacher
was convinced he would not live
to celebrate his fortieth birthday.

MAN OF THE YEAR

The world saw a cascade
of disturbing images
from a country held as a beacon
of liberty and democracy—
murders of children,
the assassination of a president
who wanted a Civil Rights Bill
to carry out what the country
had failed to deliver.
Time magazine named
Martin Luther King Jr.
Man of the Year.

Oslo, Norway
December 10, 1964

PEACE

A committee in Norway
unsettled by the violence in America
awarded Martin Luther King Jr.
the world's most prestigious award—
the Nobel Peace Prize.
They praised him for leading what many
thought impossible, a nonviolent revolution.
It was a prize for the drum major for peace,

an award for loving your enemies
no matter how many times
you and your followers
were beaten, stomped, or bombed!

1963–1964

EXPOSED

The FBI tagged Martin Luther King Jr.
the most dangerous Negro
of the future in this Nation
from the standpoint of communism,
the Negro and national security.

Its director became more outraged
when Martin received the Nobel Peace Prize,
convinced he was a communist dupe.
With Presidents Kennedy and then Johnson's approval,
Hoover had recording devices placed
in Martin's many hotel rooms.
Recordings revealed Martin had surrendered
to vanity and lust.
He had been unfaithful to Coretta.
The minister who urged obedience
to God's commandments
had broken his covenant with wife and God.

Hoover sent the recordings to Coretta.
Her reaction gave the Director little joy.

She claimed not to have recognized
her husband's voice.

Hoover applied more pressure.
Aware that young Martin
had tried to commit suicide
by jumping out a second-floor window
because he thought he had caused
his grandmother's death,
Hoover had a letter sent to Martin:
You are a colossal fraud and an evil, vicious one at that . . .
You are done. There is only one thing left for you to do.
You know what it is.

Harlem, New York
February 21, 1965

TWO GIANTS

Martin had merged his religious faith
with the nonviolent teaching
of Mohandas Gandhi.
But after a decade of protest
and the 1964 Civil Rights Bill,
Black Americans felt change
was moving too slow.
Other voices demanded more aggressive action.
A small religious sect in northern inner cities
flipped the Guardian code and color-coded
Whites as the lesser ones.

The Nation of Islam wanted
to separate, not integrate.
Malcolm X, the sect's popular minister,
ridiculed Martin for his love-thy-neighbor homilies.
Malcolm, who had replaced his last name with an X
for his unknown African name, argued:
  You don't have a turn-the-other-cheek revolution.

MALCOLM AND MARTIN

Malcolm X and Martin Luther King Jr.
posed two different answers to a question
as old as human history.
How does a person, group, or nation
fight oppression?
Retaliate with aggressive self-defense or
endure with love and pray that your suffering
changes the aggressors?
One action common, the other rare;
both take courage—
each believed theirs required more.

On a bone-cold Sunday afternoon
in a New York City ballroom
Malcolm X's wife wiggled their daughters
out of their snug snowsuits.
At precisely three o'clock
Malcolm took the stage.
The girls, excited about getting to hear
their famous daddy speak,

became annoyed when a squabble
turned their attention.
They did not see a man take
a sawed-off shotgun from beneath
his overcoat but heard the blast
that stopped their daddy's heart.

If Malcolm X, with a bevy of bodyguards
could be executed, how, pray tell,
would Martin avoid the same fate?

Selma, Alabama
March 1965

THREE DAYS

Martin was called to Alabama,
this time to a town called Selma
battling over Blacks' right to vote.
Three days tell the tale of what happened there—
Bloody Sunday
Turnaround Tuesday
and Victory Day!
Events awash in blood and death over Blacks
having a say in who should govern their lives.

Two defenders of the Lie told why Blacks
should have their citizenship rights denied:
Selma's sheriff said

largely because of their mental I.Q.
A local judge repeated the silly myth
about the connection between
intelligence and feet:
You see, most of your Selma Negroes are descended
from the Ebo [Ibo] and Angola tribes of Africa.
You could never teach or trust an Ibo back in slave days,
and even today I can spot their tribal characteristics.
They have protruding heels . . .

March 7, 1965

BLOODY SUNDAY

On the last Friday in February
twenty-six-year-old Jimmie Lee Jackson
lost his right to live, shot twice
as he stopped an Alabama State Trooper
from beating his mother, who had stopped
a trooper from beating
her eighty-two-year-old father.
Grandfather, mother, and son—
three generations—beaten, beaten,
and shot for the right to vote.

Martin agreed to lead a Sunday march
from Selma to the state capitol in Montgomery
to demand the arrest of the state trooper
who'd killed Jimmie Lee
and the right to vote in Alabama.

Six hundred gathered in front of Brown Chapel
dressed for an afternoon stroll—
not a fifty-four-mile hike.
But Martin, who promised to lead,
was a no-show. Claiming Daddy King
was sick, he had remained in Atlanta.
It caused some to wonder
if the great Martin had lost his nerve.

THE NEW CONFEDERATE ARMY

Another leader stepped forward.
Alabama-born John Lewis led
the marchers onto the Edmund Pettus Bridge
named for a Confederate brigadier general
and grand dragon of the Alabama Ku Klux Klan.
Alabama state troopers and a posse
of sheriff's deputies on horseback
waited at the crest of the bridge.
King was not there
but the lawmen didn't care.
They ordered the marchers back.
John Lewis asked for time to pray.
His kneeling was too tempting a target.
The pumped-up army could not hold back.
Before Lewis could say amen
they rained down swinging clubs and whips.
Their horses trampled
churchgoing marchers.
John Lewis, his skull fractured,

others with broken arms,
teeth, tear-gas burns
staggered back to Brown Chapel.

A television crew captured the terror;
the harrowing event was broadcast
in America and other parts of the world.
People watched the New Confederate Army
on foot and horseback push, beat, and trample
Sunday-dressed protesters on a bridge
high above the Alabama River.

JUDGE'S BAN

Turnaround Tuesday began on Monday night
when Martin sheepishly returned from Atlanta.
He didn't return alone, he'd issued a call
to churches around the country.
Ministers and rabbis came to march
with Black Alabamians
for their right to vote.

There was a problem.
Alabama had filed suit in federal court
to stop the march.
The judge had not issued a ruling.
If Martin led a march before the judge's decision
he could land in a federal prison,
and give Alabama a sure win.
But not to march? It would feed

the growing whispers
that his love-your-enemies talk
was nothing but an old
Negro preacher's dream.

HE DIDN'T

Martin made a difficult decision
and boldly told the crowd he preferred death
over betraying his conscience. He simply said
they would march, but didn't share
his risky plan.

On the Edmund Pettus Bridge
Martin, John Lewis, Ralph Abernathy,
and Black and White marchers
from all over the country
came face to face with the police.
In his solemn preacher voice
Martin announced they had
the right to march.
The state police major replied
with equal gravity:
This march will not continue.
Martin asked for time to pray and knelt.
Prayer ended without a blow.
Marchers locked arms and started to sing
"We Shall Overcome"
readied themselves for the beating
that would surely come,

prayed they had the courage.
Then Martin shocked both sides.

YES, HE DID

Martin turned and led his flock
back to the church.
He had walked a thin and risky line
but hadn't crossed it.
Kept his word and could claim
he led the march but hadn't violated
the judge's order not to march.
His critics didn't care or understand,
saw it as another sign
the Great Martin had lost his nerve.
They called it "Turnaround Tuesday."

WHITE BLOOD

That evening, four White ministers
were clubbed and kicked.
Rev. James Reeb suffered a fractured skull
too serious for the local infirmary.
He needed to be rushed to a Birmingham hospital.
The sheriff's deputies delayed the ambulance
refused to escort it on an emergency 110-mile drive.
Two days later, Rev. James Reeb of Boston,
father of four, joined Jimmie Lee Jackson
as a dead champion for Black voting rights.

WE SHALL OVERCOME

Four days after Rev. Reeb's death
Martin and others watched
President Lyndon B. Johnson
in a televised speech.
The images of Bloody Sunday
left Americans uneasy.
Johnson explained to Americans
why he'd asked Congress to pass
a Voting Rights Act that would enforce both
the Fifteenth Amendment—
which had given Black men
the right to vote in 1870—
and the Nineteenth Amendment in which
women won the same right in 1920.
President Johnson ended his speech
with words that brought tears to Martin:
It is not just Negroes,
but really it is all of us,
who must overcome
the crippling legacy
of bigotry and injustice.
And we shall overcome.

Two days later, the federal judge
handed down a decision:
The protesters had a right to march
on a federal roadway.

Martin's Turnaround Tuesday decision
to obey the judge's temporary ban had worked.
The Alabama State Police could not stop them.
The Selma to Montgomery march was on!

Victory Days!
March 21–25, 1965

WE SHALL MARCH!

In daily teams of three hundred
Blacks and Whites, old, young,
lame and strong, marched for five days
through crowds of jeering Guardians
waving Confederate flags.
At night they slept in Black homes,
farms, a hospital, and in playgrounds of Black schools.
Each morning, the march continued its protest
for the right to vote. To have a say
in who represented them.
Their cause was the same
as the American Revolution's patriots—
they were being taxed without representation.

On the final day of the march
Martin and Coretta led marchers
into Montgomery—
the city where Martin's rise
as America's Protest Preacher
had begun.
With swollen feet, Martin preached

like the Black Baptist preacher he was.
He called and responded.
He asked and answered.
How long would the Lie last
that people were color-coded
into winners and losers?
Not long!
How long would the Guardians of the Lie
hold on to their untruth?
Not long!
How long would it take to save them
from their hate?
Not long!
In front of the steps of the Alabama capitol
where the American and Confederate flags
danced in a twisted history
Martin gave his speech, calling
what the believers had come to hear.
How long before they would be treated as equals?
Not long, because no lie can live forever.

March 25, 1965

REVENGE

Another blast of hate roared
from a car window.
The Guardians struck Viola Gregg Liuzzo,
a thirty-nine-year-old White mother of five.
Inspired by Martin's dream, she'd driven
from Michigan to join the march.

On the night after the march had reached
the state capitol, she shuttled weary marchers
from Montgomery to Selma.
Returning from Montgomery with a Black colleague
she was shot to death by four Guardians,
including an FBI informant.

This news of another death
sent Martin into deeper despair.
The right of Blacks to sit
in an empty bus seat,
to eat at a lunch counter, or vote
kept the Guardians in a blood rage.
They were unwilling to be changed
by truth or love.
How long could their Lie last?
The killing of innocents
left Martin less certain
he knew the answer
no matter how many times he told others
Not long!

UP NORTH

Martin went bigger and bolder,
channeled his southern victories
into a battle with northern ghettoization.

Chicago had no legal segregation
but races lived in separate worlds
based on housing restrictions.
A half century before,
Blacks had fled Jim Crow South
and ended up in Jim Crow North.
They left their sharecroppers' cabins
moved to high-rise ghetto shacks.
Blacks held the lowest-paying jobs
made fifty-percent less than Whites
lacked the money to break the stranglehold
banks had on who got loans for housing.
Chicago laid bare the fact that race
was a national, not a southern, problem.

Martin, Coretta, and their four children
moved into Lawndale, a public housing project
in Chicago, better known as Slumdale.
Martin hoped the presence of his family
would bring attention to northern
segregated housing.

The idea of integrated housing

screeched through Chicago's
White neighborhoods like fingernails
across a blackboard.
Regardless of how many marches
were met with rocks
or how many prayer meetings
or attempts to persuade
a mayor who would never be persuaded
if he wanted to be reelected.
Martin's Chicago campaign went nowhere.

DOUBTS

Yet Martin shuttled with family in tow
between Chicago and Atlanta
for his co-pastoring duties at Ebenezer,
adding stress to his family's life.
Constant flights for fundraising to
Hollywood, New York, London
and back to Atlanta and Chicago
left his own tank near empty.
Caught in the web of his own success
he had to accept:
though he lived in Slumland
Chicago remained the most segregated
city in the North
and though he preached at Ebenezer,
Atlanta remained the most segregated
city in the South.
Neither section wanted his vision.
Older Blacks in the North continued

to doubt nonviolence would persuade
Guardians to change.
Younger Blacks saw Dr. King
as a drum major
who would march them to jail
or the graveyard.

Riverside Church
New York City
April 4, 1967

THE PROTEST PREACHER

For almost a decade as Martin
marched for peace and racial justice
the United States fought a war
in Southeast Asia.
The war had killed more
than a hundred thousand
Americans and their allies
and more than three million Vietnamese.
Yet Martin had remained silent.
After months of thought and prayer
he broadened his mission from civil rights
and denounced the Vietnam War.
His aides warned:
It would cost him the support
of President Johnson
who had persuaded Congress to pass
the Civil Rights Bill of 1964
and the Voting Rights Act of 1965.

It would turn off northern White moderates
who wanted Martin to stay in the civil rights lane.
It would unnerve older Blacks
who would fear it made them
look unpatriotic.
It would be proof to the Guardians
of why Martin Luther King Jr.
had to be stopped.
It would give the FBI another reason
to leak stories of his affairs to the press
and destroy him
quicker than a blast of dynamite.

EXPLOSION

Martin ignored them all.
He was more than a Georgia country preacher.
He was more than a Black leader.
He believed he was doing God's will.
Riverside Church in New York City
packed with listeners,
hundreds more outside
heard Martin say:
I knew that I could never again raise my voice
against the violence of the oppressed in the ghettos
without having first spoken clearly to the greatest
purveyor of violence in the world today: my own government.

President Johnson exploded:
>*What is that goddamned nigger preacher doing to me?*

BOOK THREE
1967–1968

Washington, D.C.
Summer 1967

RABBLE-ROUSER

The FBI Director ordered his agents
to start a *Rabble Rouser Index*.
One of the first names on the index
of troublemakers—people who made
comfortable Americans uncomfortable—
was Martin Luther King Jr.

America
November 1967

POOR PEOPLE'S CAMPAIGN

Martin's dream of justice
bloomed beyond race.
He realized his protests
against segregation
against the war in Vietnam
and his work for the right to vote
were not enough to change
the lives of the poor.
As long as there was poverty

regardless of race
there would be injustice.
Martin called for a March on Washington,
a Poor People's Campaign
that would bring thousands of protesters
Black and White
to demand jobs and job training
fair wages and unemployment insurance.

There were more poor Whites than Blacks,
he argued, and if there wasn't poverty
racial hatred would recede.
It was Martin Luther King Jr.'s
most expansive dream—
the end to poverty in America.

THE MOST HATED MAN

For his critics, this was the final straw.
His move from civil rights to anti-war
to freedom from poverty
was a dream too big.
In fifteen years he'd evolved
from a southern Black preacher
barely tolerated
to the most hated man in America.
A Gallup poll showed sixty-five percent
of Americans disapproved of Martin Luther King Jr.
who continued to demand more
than the country wanted to give.
To J. Edgar Hoover and many others

Martin was

the most dangerous Negro
of the future in this Nation.

Memphis, Tennessee
March 1968

MEMPHIS

A preacher friend called Martin—
another hive needed poking.
Black sanitation workers in Memphis
striking for safety and a fair wage
needed Martin's voice and prestige
to succeed.

Two workers crushed to death
in the back end of a truck.
A day of dangerous work
for a dollar an hour—
not enough to feed and house a family:
Was this a new kind of slave work?

Martin would help, yes.
His staff said no!
Plans for the March on Washington
were not going well.
But Martin heard in the Tennessee plea
the solution to his Poor People's Campaign.
A victory in Memphis would bring
more people to D.C.

Memphis, Tennessee
March 22, 1968

STORM

Martin arrived to lead workers
in a demonstration for safe machinery
and fair pay. But sixteen inches of a freakish
southern snowstorm canceled the march.

March 28, 1968

I AM A MAN

As river rats partied in ripe garbage,
and striking sanitation men draped
themselves in defiance
wearing *I AM A MAN* sandwich boards
like ancient warriors' armor,
Martin returned to lead a peaceful march.
Police wore riot gear in case he didn't.
Angry young Black men were there
to make sure he didn't.

Three sides—hope, resentment, and hate—
faced off and combusted
into looting and broken glass.
Martin rushed to a waiting car.
Everyone else was left to suffer
as riot police went to work.
One young man shot dead.

238

With tanks and loaded rifles
the National Guard took control
of the Black side of town.
Newspapers had their day criticizing
the drum major for peace and nonviolence
who had caused a riot of looting, tanks, and death.

SIDEBAR

On April 23, 1967, less than three weeks
after Martin had denounced the Vietnam War,
an unusual prison break took place
from the maximum-security
Missouri State Penitentiary.
A prisoner escaped by hiding inside
a 4-foot by 3-foot metal bakers' bread cart.
The escapee, an Army-trained rifleman,
followed Martin to Memphis
checked into the New Rebel Motel.

Morning
April 3, 1968

LORRAINE MOTEL

Because of a bomb threat,
a menace now common,
Martin's plane from Atlanta
to Memphis was grounded
but he was not stopped

from doing what he believed
was God's will. Though delayed
he returned to support
the sanitation strikers.
When he arrived
reporters, police, TV cameras,
photographers, undercover cops,
and FBI informants
escorted him to the Lorraine,
the best-known Black motel in Memphis.

Afternoon
April 3, 1968

SIDEBAR

The rifleman on his bed
at the New Rebel Motel
watched television coverage
of Martin's arrival.
He smiled as the weary
protest preacher climbed
the outdoor stairs of the Lorraine.

ANGUISH

A failure in Memphis would doom
his Poor People's Campaign.
Martin worried over the lack of
volunteers, support, and money.
He despaired over the last march,
which had not been peaceful,
was troubled with guilt over
the young man killed in the riot—
too many dying for a cause too few wanted:
racial peace and racial freedom.
Martin was distressed by hotheads
who disrupted the strikers' demands
for safe equipment and fair pay.
These young men would rather loot and run
than march with courage
and bring change by loving their enemies.

Exhausted, Martin was haunted by another worry:
the knowledge that J. Edgar Hoover
could go public with what Martin
had confessed to Coretta and hinted at
in a sermon the week before:
All of God's children were sinners
and he was a child of God.

The weather matched Martin's mood—
hard rain, wind rattling hotel windows.

The oncoming storm would keep
strikers and supporters at home.
The rally would be a bust.

DEEPER

Martin's funk did not lift.
He lacked the will and strength
to give words of hope to the workers.
He asked Ralph to take his place at the rally.
Martin remained in his room.
Rain pelted the thin windows,
lightning sparked electrical wires,
and trees snapped.
Once, he had preached:
Never lose hope.
Yet Martin was losing hope.
His agony became more intense:
He was exhausted from demonstrating.
Overwhelmed by death warnings.
He wanted to live—
not be sacrificed for the birthright
of an American citizen.

THE CALL

The telephone rang between claps of thunder.
Ralph's excitement poured through the receiver:
Mason Temple, the church for the rally,

was not full, but those who were there
were shouting Martin, Martin, Martin!
No other speaker would do.

Martin drove through the storm,
hurried inside the sweltering church.
Hearing cheers and his name chanted,
America's protest preacher strode to the pulpit
silently thanking God for this moment.
Martin Luther King Jr. did
what he was born to do:
He preached.

THE MOUNTAINTOP

Inside the hot and humid church
pounding rain sounded
like the thundering feet
of thousands who'd walked
for more than a year to prove
a Black dime was equal to a White dime.
Martin called on prayer and faith,
gave strength and hope
to striking workers:
If they held fast to their dream
they would succeed like folks
in Montgomery who'd endured
jail, death threats, and bombs,
until the Supreme Court ruled
that a Black passenger
could sit in an empty bus seat.

BELIEVE

Inside the hot and humid church
in the storm's turmoil
Martin called on prayer and faith,
gave strength and hope
to striking workers:
They would succeed
like the children
in Birmingham who suffered
mass arrests
the Bull's dogs
and water cannons—
who believed.
And Congress
passed the 1964 Civil Rights Bill
making it illegal to treat Black Americans
any different from other Americans.

HOLD FAST

In the sweltering church
sticky hot air conjured
the new Confederate Army's tear gas
choking life from the righteous
like air in the horrendous aftermath
of the Guardians' bomb
that killed four Sunday school girls.
Martin called on prayer and faith,
gave strength and hope

to the workers, telling them
to hold fast and succeed
like the folks in Selma
who had marched against nightsticks,
trampling horses, and murders.
And Congress passed the 1965
Voting Rights Act
to restore what the Guardians stole
long before:

     Black Americans' right to vote—
     the right to have a voice in their government.
     The right to decide who represented them.

THE FUTURE

Black hands waved funeral home fans
in the stifling air, and Martin startled listeners
with the unimaginable.
God had brought him
to the mountaintop
to show him the beauty
of the Promised Land.
The meaning of his message
overwhelmed him:
For the simple right of a bus seat,
toilet, or ballot, he would not live
and see the future he'd worked
to make come true.
He could not finish reciting
the "Battle Hymn of the Republic."

Words stuck in his throat:
Mine eyes have seen the glory
of the coming of the Lord . . .
As if hit by a Guardian's fist
he had to be helped to his seat.

Late afternoon
April 4, 1968

SIDEBAR

The escaped prisoner—
a Guardian rifleman—
checked out of the New Rebel Motel,
moved to a rooming house
across from the Lorraine.
With binoculars he watched
then decided he needed
a better sight line.
Stuffed the Remington Gamemaster
into its zippered case,
headed to the bathroom down the hall.
He stood in a rust-stained tub
pried open the window
waited for the target to appear,
ignoring the pounding pleas
of anyone who had to go.

6:01 p.m.

TAKE MY HAND

Across the street in Room 306
Martin, manic with joy
cleansed of his depression
from the night before
had a pillow fight
with his forever friend Ralph,
called Mama and Daddy King,
teased them both, and promised himself
to call Coretta when the kids were in bed.
It was the one-year anniversary
of his anti-Vietnam War speech
that made President Johnson
curse and pound his Oval Office desk.

Civil rights, anti-poverty, and peace
had made Martin Luther King Jr.
more protest preacher
than the country wanted.
But Martin believed he had answered
God's call and he let his thoughts drift
to what he would say
that evening at another sanitation-strike rally.
Perhaps he would start with the Bible verse
from Luke he learned as a boy from
Daddy King:
But I say unto you which hear,
Love your enemies,
do good to them which hate you.

A relaxed Martin
ten weeks into his fortieth year
stepped onto the balcony
dressed in his preacher-best suit
called to the musicians waiting below
who would perform at the evening rally
be sure and play:
"Precious Lord, take my hand."

The Guardians' sharpshooter squeezed
the cold trigger and a single bullet
exploded on contact.
Martin's shocked body crossed over to death.
The drum major for peace, murdered
for his dream that love could conquer hate.

America
April 4, 1968

THE BATTLE HYMN

The evening Martin died
many mourned, some rioted
but few understood
he had snapped the shackles
of Black mental enslavement
and set free many White Guardians
from the Lie of racial superiority.

In his sermon the night before
he could not finish reciting
"The Battle Hymn of the Republic,"
the Civil War song that asked abolitionists
of Frederick Douglass and Harriet Tubman's days
to give their lives for the slave:
    Let us die to make men free.
Martin Luther King Jr. gave his life
in an attempt to make America free
of racial ignorance and arrogance.

IN THE END

MEMORY

Martin Luther King Jr. was the voice
of the civil rights movement
that transformed the country
and changed how he is remembered.
Martin went from
the most dangerous Negro
in the country
to a national holiday.
Today his statue rises from the Stone of Hope
near the National Mall.
Songs, movies, and books sculpt him
as they tell and retell his story.
Street signs bear his name
but mostly in Black neighborhoods.
School assemblies and city halls
celebrate and airbrush the bombings,
beatings, dog bites, killings
carried out by the Guardians of the Lie
in the name of Jim Crow segregation,
White supremacy, southern heritage,
and northern acceptance of a racial ladder.
The inspirational words he often sang
  We shall overcome
drown out the painful failure of
  We shall live in peace someday.

250

Hidden too are Martin's flaws
and the real meaning of his dream—
a nonviolent country free of
poverty
racism
and war
where all are equal under the law.

MLK DAY

On the next Martin Luther King Day
when his memory makes its annual
January school visits and overstays
for February's Black History Month
remember the grit and courage he showed
the mental price paid
forgiveness needed
honor deserved
not as a Black History icon
but as an American prophet
who dreamed of a time
greater than the one he lived.

PERSONAL HISTORY

Every school morning I pledged allegiance
. . . *to the Flag of the United States of America,*
and to the Republic for which it stands,
one Nation under God . . .
In the Army, I defended the promise
of our corrected Constitution.
Every game night, I stand and sing
"The Star-Spangled Banner."
But every now and then, a headline
knocks me backward
forces me to regain my confidence
restore my faith that the poem
my mother turned into a prayer
to get us through the day
will come true:

> *Besides,*
> *They'll see how beautiful I am*
> *And be ashamed—*
> *I, too am America.*

PART III

1961–2008

The Promise of America

BARACK OBAMA
1961-

The Audacity of Race

My identity might begin with the fact of my race, but it didn't, couldn't end there.

—Barack Obama

Jakarta, Indonesia
April 9, 1968

PASSING THE TORCH

On the day of Martin Luther King Jr.'s
funeral, halfway around the world,
six-year-old Barry Obama—
the son of an American
mother and African father—
wondered if there would be a day
when he would be judged
by the content of his character
not the color of his skin.

THE IMPOSSIBLE MADE POSSIBLE

The question from the start
how did the United States
with its history of race
elect Barack Obama president?
His Black African father from Kenya,
son of the Luo tribe.
His White American mother, Kansas-born,
daughter of the Scottish-Irish tribe.
His Brown stepfather from Indonesia,
an island nation between the Indian
and Pacific oceans.
This second marriage carried his mother,
studying in Hawaii, and six-year-old
Barry Obama from Honolulu to Jakarta.

How did America with its racial history
and *this* family history
elect Barack Hussein Obama
who had immigration, race, and the world
stamped on his *coffee with cream* face?
It was the question from the start.

257

CHILD BARRY

Awake hours before his Catholic
schoolmates in Muslim Jakarta
Barry received a daily breakfast
of how to think and write from
his mother Stanley Ann:
  a bowl of English grammar
  mixed with American history
  sprinkled with the fruits of Dr. King's marches
  to nourish Barry's American roots.

Lolo, his stepfather, taught different lessons:
  how to bring down the street bully
  how the world respects the strong
  who take from the weak—
  lessons Lolo learned in New Guinea
  where leeches sucked blood
  from inside his army boots—
  lessons Mom did not want her son to learn.

Mixed in her early morning teachings
Stanley Ann added stories of Barry's father's
rise from a Kenyan hut
to university degrees, vaulting
over the brute and muscle-bound.
Another way to be strong.

THE RIDDLE

Age nine, Barry's shaken
by a magazine story or a nightmare
image of a man who peeled blackness
from his skin, changed his face
to the color of stale white bread
the width of his nose unchanged
his hair still African-curled
his eyes circled in regret.
What drove the man to bleach his skin?
What problem did he solve
in his laboratory of self-hate?

Barry stood before a mirror
searched for answers.
Were there clues in his calabash features?
African-tough hair, caramel-colored skin
darker than his mother's, lighter than his father's?
In the privacy of his mind
a riddle taunted
why is race such a heavy rock to carry?

FIFTH GRADE

Barry needed a better school,
Stanley Ann a better marriage.
She sent ten-year-old Barry
back to Hawaii to live with her parents.
She stayed in Jakarta with Lolo
and their daughter, Baby Maya.

Barry, a scholarship kid
at a prestigious academy,
was often asked about his name
a less-than-subtle demand
to confess his race.
Classmates, more White than otherwise,
displayed their worldly knowledge
with monkey sounds and a pestering question.
Which cannibals, Africans or Indonesians,
had the sharpest teeth?
Barry spun a lie—
his father, an African prince
his grandfather, a king.
Both gave Barry the right to be
among the privileged and bright.

Honolulu, Hawaii
Christmas 1971

REUNION

Stanley Ann, Baby Maya, Barry
and grandparents Toot and Gramps
planned a Christmas reunion in Hawaii.
Word came that Barry's father
was coming too
whiskey-breath Gramps exhaled
  Should be one hell of a Christmas.
Barry's thoughts stampeded
what should he expect from the man
he didn't know, his father?

Barack Obama Sr. hadn't seen
his son since he was an infant.
Now a Kenyan government official,
charismatic man of the world
slender with malaria-yellowed eyes
set in a dark Black face,
walked with a limp
returned to Hawaii
to recuperate after a car accident
was the story he told.

THE MARRIAGE

The story not told:
Barry's father
romanced his mother
when she was seventeen,
a college freshman who'd never
had a serious boyfriend.

They married before baby Barry arrived.
Quiet wedding, no family present
on another island where the marriage
would not be reported in the Honolulu papers
would not require Toot and Gramps to explain
their son-in-law's last name.

Bride and groom returned blushing
from their wedding
she to her parents' house,
he to his student quarters.
Stanley Ann had turned eighteen
dashing Barack Senior twenty-four
or twenty-six, from a land
where multiple wives were the custom
and year of births was not.
He had a wife and two children in Kenya.
Six months later Barry was born
in a Honolulu maternity ward.

REUNION BOMB

In his grandparents' crowded apartment
Barry watched the drama play out.
The actors were Kansas White,
African Black, and blended Brown.
Tensions had nothing to do with race or color
but with family strife and love.

Barack Sr. sat in grumpy Gramps's favorite chair.
Toot mumbled from the kitchen
nobody was helping with the dishes.
Stanley Ann avoided her parents' warning stares
rocked her second husband's baby.
Tensions wound tighter,
Barry's father exploded—
      Barry watches too much television!
Ordered his son to do homework
teachers had not assigned.
His mother came to console,
dropped a bomb instead.
Barry's teacher had invited his dad
to speak to his class.
Barry's lie
being the son of a prince
ready to explode.

GUEST SPEAKER

The morning of reckoning arrived.
His father in front of the room
where the teacher should be,
a map of East Africa pulled down,
the class next door crowded in
along the walls eager to hear
an African speak.

Eyes bounced from Barry to father
pondering differences, seeking similarities.
Barry fretted. Which would come first,
being embarrassed by his father
or the princely lie exposed?

Barack Sr. began. Students listened
at first polite, then more engaged
as he spun a beguiling tale
that started in the Great Rift Valley
where all humans evolved
moved to the many Kenyan tribes,
some of whom lived in shining city buildings,
to goat herders living in huts
and those who required their sons
to go to the bush and spear a lion.
He closed his tale with Kenyans
overthrowing British colonial rule
like the Americans two centuries before.
The class sat in awe and applauded,

regretted their monkey and cannibal teasing.
His father had charmed them all.
Barry felt princely proud. His tall tale survived.

A PROMISE MADE

Reunion over, Barry's parents
packed their bags
grandparents panic-worried
mother crying but refused
to be wife number four.

Barack Sr. returned to Kenya,
Stanley Ann and Baby Maya to Jakarta.
Brown Barry stayed in Asian-tan Hawaii
with his Kansas White grandparents
after his parents flew west
in different directions.

Barry, a kid of ten,
made a promise without words.
He would take from his father
the self-confidence he showed Barry's class:
      command of language and facts
      sharpness of mind that persuaded
      others to like him.
Barry would reject from his father
      the thorns that aged his grandparents
      and made his mother cry.

RACE

Barry reached eleventh grade.
Letters between father and son
dwindled to a hurtful silence.
Stanley Ann returned home
a single mom once again
supporting Barry and Maya
on a small budget while she studied
anthropology at the University of Hawaii.

Barry, a half-Black kid in an Asian White
private school had to figure out how to
   raise myself to be a Black man in America.

His everydays showed the challenge
of being Black was not cured
by the civil rights movement.
The country had changed
but the consequences of race
roamed free.
   The seventh-grader who called
   him a name and couldn't understand
   why Barry bloodied his nose.

   The tennis coach who warned
   I shouldn't touch the schedule
   pinned up on the bulletin board
   because my color might rub off.

266

The lack of Black girls at school
and the refusal of Whites and Asians
to return his calls.

The unease of being one
of the few Blacks at school parties
standing aloof against the wall.

The unease of White friends
he took to a Black party
at the nearby army base.

The clowning of classmates
who greeted him in hip street talk,
or tried to copy the court moves
of NBA superstars.

And worst of all, squirming
when a Black friend complained
about Whites, but exempted
Barry's mom and grandparents.

Insults, mild compared to the suffering
of earlier generations, but stinging
like fifth-grade monkey calls
showing Barry he was an outsider
feeding his urgency to solve the riddle
how to be Black without rejecting
his White family?
How to be Black in America
but not defined by race?

CHARLIE

Barry went through the motions
of school, getting above-average
grades now and then.
He found refuge in booze and weed.
His fellow smokers, Asian, Black,
and White, joined him
in a mutual discontent.
No questions about family or race,
the smoky shield protected him
from solving the riddle.

Stanley Ann worried Barry
was too casual about his future,
at risk of becoming a *good-time Charlie*.
A good-time what? A good-time Charlie.
A loafer.
Barry struck back and regretted
his words: *Look at Gramps.*

His mom flinched. Her father,
Stanley, who named her after himself,
was a man of many dreams
he failed to reach.
Barry watched his mother tear up
and knew he had broken his promise
not to make his mother cry.

BECOMING BARACK

He studied a bit more
caused his mom less grief
casually filled out college applications
graduated from high school
chose Occidental College
near Los Angeles.
Why?
Because he met a girl
on a Honolulu beach
who lived near the college.
It was a spring flirtation
that disappeared by fall
when he landed in L.A.

Around cafeteria tables, on library steps
warmed by the California sun,
or in dorm rooms littered with beer bottles,
where music blasted through walls and air reeked of weed,
the question nagged, how not to be stunted by race
and Barry could not let it go.

When he sat with the Black "tribe"
the lunch table bounced with laughter
the loud sound of freedom to be themselves
rather than a group of Black students.

When he sat with biracial students
like him, they talked of being an individual,
preened their light-skin looks
and avoided other Blacks.

When he sat with self-claimed "thinkers"
a cabal of Latinos, Whites, and Blacks
the air was filled with political readings
and social justice chatter.

With each group, the question of race
appeared in different guises—
How to be Black but not defined by race?

Then a young woman asked
why he was called Barry, not Barack?
The question startled. As if being told
he wore an ill-fitted shirt and should change
into something more comfortable.

SOUTH AFRICA

Newly named Barack became active
in the college's South African
anti-apartheid movement.
The African country with a Black majority
segregated and dominated by the White minority
who imprisoned anti-apartheid's leader, Nelson Mandela,
for wanting Black Africans to have a say
in how their country was governed.

Barry stood on an outdoor stage
on a beautiful autumn afternoon
and made his first political speech:
Barack shouted of a race struggle
halfway around the world
that resonated inside himself.

New York City
1981–1983

A CALL FROM KENYA

Barack smoked and drank less
thought and studied more.
Transferred to Columbia University
in New York City at the edge
of Black and Spanish Harlem
where names and faces were a grab bag
of the world's people.

What to do after college?
Unclear.
Perhaps a visit to Kenya
to get to know his father
man to man.
He wrote him for the first time
in many years, made plans for a visit.
Then came the call
that spun Barack back.
His father was dead.
Car accident.

He called his mom,
shared the tragedy
heard the cry for her son
who had lost his father.
But Barack felt no pain
for the man he didn't know.

COMMUNITY ORGANIZER

Barack took a job that soon turned sour
working in a New York City high-rise
writing reports to help the rich grow richer.

His outer appearance—a young man
beginning a prosperous career.
On the inside, more like his mom—
an anthropologist who helped
Indonesian women start craft businesses
to better their lives.
Barack dreamed the same—
find a way to help others
better their lives.
Black secretaries and a security guard
in his high-rise company
saw in him what they wished
for their children—a person of color
at the starting line of success.
They urged him not to waste
his chance to be one of their own
who was successful and rich.

He kept his own counsel,
continued his search.
Chicago had elected its first
Black mayor, and Barack thought
the city might be the place for him.
He applied for a job with the mayor
and social organizations.
Only two expressed interest
in the young college grad with
a funny last name.
The first, persuading rich donors
to give money to a civil rights organization.
The second paid little,
a community organizer.
Barack accepted the second
and headed for Chicago.

Chicago
1985–1988

COMMUNITY

Barack took a job few wanted,
community organizer
on Chicago's South Side.
The Developing Communities Project,
funded by White suburban churches,
led by a Jewish man working to lift
poor Blacks from their color-coded despair
in a city changing from White to Black
or something in between.

THE CHALLENGE

The enormity of what he faced
slow-walked Barack to the consequences of race:
  jobs that did not earn a living
  schools that did not lead to employment
  public housing that did not nurture self-worth
  unsafe and crumbling neighborhoods
  that trapped and traumatized in a cycle
  created and sustained by governments, customs,
  and preferences for a color-coded society.

He heard the prayers and lamentations
filter from once-regal churches
and iron-gated gospel storefronts.
The longing for hope, respect, and a way out
of a life pressed by the two-century-old
gravitational force of race
still pressing life from the powerless.

THE GARDENS

Two thousand apartments
in a bramble of bricked low-rises
sheltered Chicago's unwanted.
A public housing nightmare
with a dreamy name, Altgeld Gardens.
Set between a large, rat-infested

field and a sewage-treatment plant
that spewed an epidemic of asthma.
The Gardens' old pipes were wrapped
in suspected asbestos—a material
whose flaking particles penetrated lungs
and added to the Gardens' respiratory ills.

The forgotten people in the Gardens
mostly single moms and grandmothers
prayed for the safety and future
of the children as they witnessed
hope and ambition drained
from their innocent eyes.

Barack took a small step to change
a small piece of the world,
organized a campaign to force
Chicago Public Housing to test
for asbestos contamination.
He led a party of eight who demanded
to speak to the director
of the Chicago Public Housing Authority.
The receptionist cold and unimpressed
by the skinny community organizer
and his ragtag committee from the Gardens
   asked them to leave
   threatened to call security.
   Then the press arrived.

An assistant to an assistant manager
magically appeared, invited them

into a conference room, where the press
could not follow, and promised to test
the buildings for asbestos.

A small victory by the community organizer
who planned each step:
>renting the bus that carried them
>downtown
>prepping the speaker to demand testing
>alerting the press.
It was a small answer toward the bigger question:
>*Do we settle for the world as it is,*
>*or do we work for the world as it should be?*

THE GHOST

Barack's half-sister from Kenya, Auma,
paid him a ten-day visit
to meet the brother
their father had bragged about.
As Auma spoke, Barack
became reflective and gloomy
as the ghost of their father
danced between them.

Barack Sr.'s Christmas visit
to Honolulu fourteen years earlier
had been a trip of desperation.
After a drunken car accident
that left the other driver dead,
he spent a year in the hospital

and lost his job.
Wife number three, Ruth,
a Boston schoolteacher
who'd followed him
to Kenya, bore him two children but
divorced him when she discovered
he'd fathered *another* son
with wife number one.

Barack had turned his father
into royalty, a man who had used
the power of his brain
to rise from an African hut
to become a man of the Western world.
But in the end, he was broken and lost.

Their father's trip to Hawaii
had been a wild promise he made to Auma
to bring Stanley Ann and Barry
to Kenya and become a new family.

Barack Sr. returned alone
struggled to reset his life
begged his way into a low-level job
in the government he despised.
Tried to outrun some unknown pain
until he accelerated his drinking
and wrapped his car
around an unforgiving tree
and lay buried in his stepmother's backyard.

WANTING SOMETHING MORE

Strings of good-luck balloons
an array of goodbyes
marked the end of Barack's
three-year stay in Chicago,
the first time he had lived
in a Black community.
He'd found acceptance
found purpose and place
felt he belonged
but ready to grow.

Barack the community organizer
had more failures than successes
but in the housing projects,
barbershops, juke joints,
churches, and around kitchen tables
he received more than he gave.

With a law degree
he thought he could solve
greater problems.
If elected to public office
he could correct the corrosive consequences
of being Black in America.

LAND OF HIS FATHERS

Barack flew to Kenya with a simple
and difficult goal:
I could somehow force my many worlds
into a single, harmonious whole.
His mother's family, his life in Hawaii and Chicago
were painted squares of a rotating cube.
To click his father's squares into place
might make his many worlds align.

Auma welcomed him "home,"
introduced him to his father's world
at dinners and celebrations
with curious half-siblings, aunts, and uncles.
He stayed in Auma's apartment
visited his father's sister Sarah
lunched with his half-brother Mark
and Mark's mother Ruth,
the American woman
who had followed Barack's father
from Boston and became wife number three.
Later he took an overnight train
to Granny's, a hedged-in compound,
and listened to her stories—
the painted squares
of his father's life clicked into place.
It was not a harmonious whole.

THE GRAVES

In Granny's backyard, Barack knelt before
his grandfather's grave:
Hussein Onyango Obama.
His father's grave, covered with chipped
bathroom tiles, bore no name.

Granny told what Barack's two namesakes
had faced, what damaged them
in their struggle to live in the land
as it changed from old Africa
to an oppressed British colony
and then to a new and independent
nation far from perfect.

Hussein Onyango, Barack's grandfather,
was overly proud of the English ways
acquired when he worked in Nairobi
and in Burma as a British army cook.
He traded his loincloth for pants,
rode a bicycle, owned a radio that filled
his hut with scratchy London voices.
It wasn't the color of English whiteness
he admired but their power:
the force of their rifles
their cunning to take the land
and bend its people to their will.
Barack's grandfather was mean
and strict with his wives and children
if they did not follow his British ways.

Barack's grandmother ran away
and left her children:
twelve-year-old Sarah,
nine-year-old Barack Sr.

The children went to find her
spent weeks in the countryside
hiding, stealing food, and drinking
from muddy streams before being discovered.
Their mother never returned.

BARACK SENIOR

With Granny's words, Barack learned
how his father had been beaten
told he was not good enough
yet became a bright student
who could ace tests
but found life harder than university.
At age forty-eight he left eight children
from four mothers.

Barack knelt at his father's
unmarked grave. A destructive life
covered in thrown-away bathroom tiles.
Being brilliant was not enough—
a life had to be anchored in self-worth.

HARVARD LAW

Barack returned from Kenya
a more serious person.
In a class of the brightest
at the toughest law school
he was older, and professors
knew he was exceptional.
Classmates called him
> *This voice of authority*
> *The Great Obama.*

When questions were asked
Barack's hand went up first
with answers long and involved.
Others were glad he ran down the clock
and kept them from being called upon.

Chicago
Summer 1989

MEET THE INTERN

Summer break sent Barack,
an overeager Harvard intern,
to a top-tier Chicago firm
where a promising young lawyer
would mentor him.

Michelle Robinson had Princeton and Harvard
diplomas on her wall, blue ribbons
testifying drive and seriousness.
She was a child from Chicago's Black South Side
breathing the rarefied air of corporate
law on Chicago's Other Side.

The mentor found the mentee unusual.
He didn't doubt himself. As weeks passed,
Barack proved why, and their respect
for each other grew.
When the summer was over
they remained friends and in time became more.

Harvard Law
Cambridge, Massachusetts
1991

IMPROVING LIVES

Barack was elected president
of the *Harvard Law Review*
the highest honor a law student could receive
and was contracted by a publisher
to write his memoir—
the story of his young life—
an unusual honor even for someone
as unusual as Barack.
He graduated magna cum laude,
the usual award for an exceptional student.

On graduation day students packed
their bags and left for high-paying jobs
in glass-tower buildings,
to pay back student loans
and have money left over.
Barack had seen the poor in Jakarta,
New York, Kenya, and Chicago.
With his law degree ready
to hang on the wall
he wanted to improve the lives
of the powerless.

Self-assured and determined
he headed to Chicago
to be with Michelle and thrive
as husband and wife
as his parents never had.

Chicago
1992–1995

FAMILY

Barack and Michelle were married
in October 1992.
Two daughters were born
Malia in '98,
Sasha in '01.
Barack had what his parents wanted—
a family.

In the middle of his first election spin in 1995
to win a seat in the Illinois state senate
his mother was diagnosed with cancer.
Barack made two trips to visit her
a third was booked but too late—
Stanley Ann died holding Maya's hand.
Barack grieved he wasn't there
to hold the other hand of his mother
who had braved an unconventional life
anchored him in self-worth
>to be a loving husband
>to becoming a loving parent
and show him
how to step beyond the limits of race.

POLITICS

Reelected three times as a state senator
eager to run on a faster track
the U.S. House of Representatives
but knocked to the side of the road.

Barack's hope hardwired
ready to run again
blessed with Michelle Obama
as exceptional as himself.
Together their appeal, astonishing and fresh
attracted thousands and eventually millions
who believed in the promise of America.

Competitors thought this upstart
community organizer
turned lawyer turned politician
didn't have a chance.
Barack showed voters White and Black
he would serve on their behalf
heard their common hope for respect
a better life for their kids.
Barack Obama, in 2004,
U.S. Senator from Illinois.

Springfield, Illinois
February 10, 2007

YES, WE CAN

Senate work, national speeches
handshaking, network-building
Barack lifted his eyes to the top of the pole
saw what he wanted, thought he could reach it
knew he was capable.
The country's full of people of goodwill
who would see him as able, likable, trustable.
He was ready for the White House.

Are you kidding?
Don't you know American race history?
Michelle, less than thrilled, knew the risks
of thrusting daughters into the harsh limelight
knew the danger of deranged crackpots
and born-again supremacists wanting the rub of fame.

286

THE LAND OF LINCOLN

In 2007, in Springfield
where Abraham Lincoln had lived
where race riots of 1908
had left two Black men hanging from trees
where Whites shouted
> *Lincoln freed you,*
> *now we'll show you*
> *where you belong.*

Barack believed the country was not static.
The civil rights movement
with its twin pillars of hope
the Civil Rights Act of 1964
and the Voting Rights Act of 1965
had profoundly changed America.
Barack was running for president!

The press and the cable talking heads
quickly pointed out the junior senator
was *not* ready:
A Black president? Time's *not* right.
The name, Barack Hussein Obama, *not* great!
It would remind voters of Osama bin Laden's
al-Qaeda nightmare of September 11, 2001
when three thousand Americans perished.

Some opponents in his own party
saw no need to worry.
They knew the American mind
perhaps one day, but not today.

Don't be discouraged, they might have said
and maybe they would invite him
to be in their Cabinet,
Secretary of this or that
when they became president.
Other politicians in his party
saw Barack as extraordinary,
someone who could surf
the rising tide made possible
by the Voting Rights Act of 1965
and the country's changing attitudes.
They encouraged him to run.
Now is the time!

*Presidential Campaign
2007–2008*

THE FACE OF RACE

It had happened before.
Black women and men ran for president
but none were thought to have a chance.
Too many voters were stuck
in the glue trap of race.
Candidates didn't know how to pry them free.

Barack was unusual; the times were different.
As a U.S. senator from Illinois
he'd won votes in large Black and White cities
and small White farming towns.
He showed he understood the need

to serve the voter, to see
beyond the face of race
to the things that made
their lives more secure.

On the presidential campaign
Barack didn't talk about race,
he focused on the economy,
how Americans needed help
keeping their jobs and homes
having health care and better schools.
Many agreed with what Barack was saying.
They heard someone who understood
what was important to them.

But RACE in America is an open sore
never allowed to heal.
His opponents saw it as a weapon
to bring him down.

"BIRTHERISM"

Barack's popularity continued to rise.
To derail his charm and appeal
a lie was hatched that was so far-fetched
he thought it couldn't be a threat.
The U.S. Constitution requires
a President to be a natural-born citizen
at least thirty-five years old
a resident of the country
for the last fourteen years.

Barack met those requirements
but a rumor that he was not American-born
picked up speed.

At first Barack ignored the rolling boulder
as a crazy-boy prank
a race-baiting game too inane
for anyone to believe that he
wasn't born where his mother gave birth.
More and more people believed the lie.
Barack posted his birth record
on his website to put an end
to the comedy hoax.
Conspirators' eyes glittered
in prankster's glee, called the certificate
FAKE!

Chicago, Illinois
March 2008

SHARKS CIRCLED

Not satisfied with the birth hoax
race baiters found another way
to pump the race scare.
The Reverend Jeremiah Wright
of Chicago's Trinity United Church of Christ
had befriended Barack years before
when he was a community organizer

helped him become a man of faith
married him and Michelle
baptized Malia and Sasha.

Reverend Wright was an ex-marine
and an over-the-top preacher
who lifted his parishioners in amens and joys.
He preached God's love for the downtrodden
        soothed the spirit of the ghetto-trapped,
        pulled them back from the edge of despair,
        helped them endure the cross of injustice,
        alleviated the pain of their daily lives.

Barack's savvy opponent turned
the fiery preacher into a poster child
of the angry Black man who hated America
and Whites, so a video claimed.

The good Reverend said
some wild and crazy things.
He damned America, said the government
had conspired to infect Black people with HIV,
said the September 11 al-Qaeda attack
was payback for America's actions around the world.
Sharks circled Barack's campaign
smelling blood in the water.

If the Reverend was an angry Black man
who hated Whites, then Obama was anti-American,
anti-White, and unfit to be president.
Lies that brought his campaign to a halt

forced Barack to do what he wanted to avoid
talk about race in America, a topic too raw
for a calm and thoughtful discussion.

March 18, 2008

"A MORE PERFECT UNION"

"The Meaning of July Fourth for the Negro"
lifted Frederick Douglass to the Great Hall
of American Memory.
"I Have a Dream" put Martin Luther King
near the National Mall.
And not far from where Ona Judge
had fled George Washington's toothy frown
two blocks from Independence Hall
where "We the People" echoed,
Barack gave a speech:
said the Constitution was
> *stained by this nation's original sin of slavery*
but
> *at its very core* [was] *the ideal of equal citizenship*
> *under the law . . .*
From slavery to civil rights,
Americans of goodwill had
> *to narrow that gap*
> *between the promise of our ideals*
> *and the reality of their time.*
Each generation had to
> *continue the long march . . .*

THE COMPLEXITIES OF RACE

Barack did not blink or fail to admit
that the video snippets of Reverend Wright's
angered Whites and Blacks.

He explained that Reverend Wright
was a man of his times
when Jim Crow lynchings and discrimination
strangled and suppressed Black lives.
The good Reverend was unable
to free himself from that ugly history
or the pain of those he served
who still suffered on Chicago's Black Side.

Barack's vision was for a new unity.
To achieve it, America had to acknowledge
the audacity of race.

Chicago, Illinois
November 4, 2008

THE EXTRA ORDINARY

Barack's extraordinary touch
led people to scrape old beliefs
from the soles of their shoes.
What many thought was impossible
the voting majority made possible.

It was an extra ordinary time
that paused the trauma of slavery
and soothed the unhealed scars of Jim Crow
inflicted by the audacity of race.

It was an extra ordinary time
an extraordinary person
caused so many to ignore
born-again supremacists' punch card of lies
Barack Hussein Obama is:

    A foreign citizen
    A Muslim and anti-Christian
    A radical Black Christian who is anti-American
    An African Islamist who is anti-White.

The votes rolled in on that November night:

    96 percent of Black voters
    66 percent of young voters
    53 percent of all voters
    43 percent of White voters
    365 Electoral College votes
    Elected
Barack Obama, President of the United States.

A LONG TIME COMING

Cheers refused to go silent.
Bright lights chased
chill from November's night air.
Smiles of the next First Family
in front of large American flags
warmed Chicago's Grant Park.
President-elect Barack Obama,
the dream of hope, a man of smarts
waved to the near quarter of a million
who couldn't believe the impossible had happened!
Cheers grew louder as he spoke:
> *It's been a long time coming . . .*

BARACK KNEW

*I will never forget
that in no other country on Earth
is my story even possible.*

He Also Knew
> His election was but a chapter
> in the long story to free the country
> from the corrosive consequences of race.
> Better chapters would be written
> by future generations.

THEN AND NOW

A new day dawned on a cold Tuesday afternoon
  Sweet land of liberty
rang from Aretha Franklin's church-holy voice
  My country, 'tis of thee
warmed almost two million
  Land of the pilgrims' pride
stretched from the Capitol to the National Mall
  My heart with rapture fills
floated a fever of joy across the world's screens
  Of thee I sing
The impossible made possible, hope made real.
  Let freedom ring
Words Harriet Tubman refused to sing on Jubilee Day—
the Emancipation Proclamation did not free her Maryland
people—
now she's honored in the Military Intelligence Corps Hall of
Fame
for keeping the Union free.
  Sweet land of liberty
Ida B. Wells showed the world Jim Crow's horrors—
now posthumously awarded the Pulitzer Prize, the highest
honor in journalism in the United States.
  Land where my fathers died
Martin Luther King's statue stands nearby.
  Let music swell the breeze

Frederick Douglass's statue greets tourists
in the United States Capitol Visitor Center.
    Sweet freedom's song
Ona Judge once enslaved in the President's House.
    Let all that breathe partake
Barack Obama elected to the White House.
    Sweet land of liberty
My country 'tis of all of us.

EPILOGUE

THE LONG TIME

1796

Ona, not a Judge, but a
Thief.
Did not wait to hear liberty's
Bell.
Stole what she could not have—
Herself.
It was a long time coming.

1838

Frederick Douglass's lightning
Mind.
Did not wait for Union's
Victory.
Sparked freedom from heaven's
Stars.
It was a long time coming.

1849

Harriet Tubman fearless
Warrior.
Did not wait for Lincoln's

Proclamation.
Guided the unfree with her North Star's
Torch.
It was a long time coming.

1892

Ida B. Wells, citizens'
Crusader.
Did not wait to expose
Jim Crow.
Showed the world his brutal
Crimes.
It was a long time coming.

1955

Martin Luther King Jr., America's protest
Preacher.
Did not wait for the Guardians'
Repentance.
Marched evil from the country's
Promise.
It was a long time coming.

2009

Barack Obama, United States
President.

Did not wait for racial hate to
Clear.
Challenged the Guardians to
Change.
It was a long time coming.

Today

Ona to Obama, red, white, and blue
Sparks.
Did not wait for others to light the
Sky.
Declared a new Fourth of
July.
It was a long time coming.

Tomorrow

You, you, and you,
Friend.
Do not wait. Their work is not yet
Done.
Push *We the people* beyond the founders'
Vision.
It was a long time coming.

THE LONG STRUGGLE
To Form a More Perfect Union

The Long Time
a perpetual challenge
to agree who the
WE
should be
in *We the people*
to form a more perfect Union.
Thee but not me
Me but not thee
OR
You and Me together
without a hyphen in between?

1775–1783

The American Revolutionary War—Five thousand Blacks,
free and enslaved, serve in the Continental Army under
the command of General George Washington. The thirteen
American colonies defeat the British Army and establish the
United States of America.

1776

The Declaration of Independence is signed, proclaiming *that all
men are equal* (although all thirteen colonies allowed slavery).
It refers to the original inhabitants, Native Americans, as
merciless Indian Savages.

1788

The U.S. Constitution is ratified. The word *slavery* is not used;

instead, enslaved people are considered property and referred to as "persons held to Service or Labour." Article I, Section 2—for purposes of representation and taxes, Black slaves were counted as three-fifths compared to one free person (White or Black). Section 2 of Article IV required that any enslaved person who escaped to another state must be returned.

1790
The Naturalization Act declares that only free White people can become naturalized citizens of the United States.

1793
The first Fugitive Slave Act prevents any slave that escapes to a free state from being declared free and requiring return to their owner.

1796
Ona Judge escapes. Because of the first Fugitive Slave Act, she is a fugitive—not a free person.

1808
The Act Prohibiting Importation of Slaves as required in the U.S. Constitution that barred international slave trade goes into effect (Article I, Section 9). However, it spurs the domestic slave trade.

1812–1815
The United States battles against Great Britain in the War of 1812. One-sixth of the U.S. Navy is Black. The war reaffirmed American independence, but slavery continued for another half-century.

1838

Frederick Douglass escapes. Because of the first Fugitive Slave Act he is a fugitive, not a free person.

1849

Harriet Tubman escapes. Because of the first Fugitive Slave Act she is a fugitive, not a free person.

1850

The second Fugitive Slave Act becomes law. It requires everyone to help slave catchers and sets up special commissioners to implement the new law.

1857

The Dred Scott Decision—the U.S. Supreme Court rules that African Americans are not citizens but property and have no rights to sue.

1859

John Brown and twenty-one men raid the U.S. military arsenal at Harpers Ferry, Virginia, with the goal of inciting a slave revolt. Brown is captured and executed. Frederick Douglass is accused of being a co-conspirator and flees to England to escape arrest.

1861–1865

Confederate Secession—eleven slave states declare their independence and form the Confederate States of America, with plans to establish a large slave empire. Secession ignites the Civil War, and following defeat of the Confederates, American slavery ends with the ratification of Thirteenth Amendment.

1863

Emancipation Proclamation declares freedom for Confederate slaves, but not Union slaves in Delaware, Maryland, Kentucky, Missouri, Tennessee counties under Union control—and West Virginia when it becomes a state in June 1863. The proclamation allows Blacks to serve in the Union Army.

1863–1865

Nearly 200,000 Blacks serve in the Union Army and Navy during the Civil War.

1865

President Abraham Lincoln is assassinated three days after suggesting that Blacks who fought for the Union should have the right to vote.

1865

On June 19, in Galveston, Texas, Union General Gordon Granger reads the Emancipation Proclamation and announces to his Black audience that they were no longer slaves. This day is celebrated as Juneteenth, a national holiday.

1865

The Thirteenth Amendment abolishes slavery in the United States and its territories.

1865

In response to the Thirteenth Amendment abolishing slavery, the Ku Klux Klan (KKK), a White nationalist group, forms in Pulaski, Tennessee.

1865–1950

An estimated 6,500 people were victims of racial terror murders between the end of the Civil War and the beginning of the civil rights movement.

1865–1965

Jim Crow statutes, a series of state and local rules, are enacted to restrict the rights of African Americans.

1867

Congress passes the first Reconstruction Act over President Andrew Johnson's veto. The former Confederate states are placed under military occupation until they meet conditions for readmittance to the Union, e.g., equal protection of the laws.

1868

Fourteenth Amendment declares all people except Native Americans, born or naturalized in the United States, to be American citizens. The amendment also grants equal "protection of the laws," a provision that goes largely unenforced.

1870

Fifteenth Amendment to the U.S. Constitution is ratified, granting Black men the right to vote. But the Amendment is not enforced in southern states.

1875

The Civil Rights Act is enacted by Congress to protect the rights of Blacks to equal treatment in public accommodations and public transportation and the right to serve on juries. State and federal governments do not enforce the Act. The law is declared unconstitutional in 1883.

1877
The Hayes-Tilden Compromise: Rutherford B. Hayes of Ohio wins the 1876 presidential election and becomes the nineteenth president. He promises that federal troops will be withdrawn from the former Confederate states and Black citizenship rights will no longer be protected by the federal government.

1882
The Chinese Exclusion Act restricts the immigration of Chinese to the United States.

1892
Ida B. Wells publishes *Southern Horrors*, exposing the use of lynching to suppress African American citizenship rights.

1896
In *Plessy v. Ferguson*, the Supreme Court rules that racial segregation, if the services are equal, does not violate the Constitution. The decision allows for segregated schools and public accommodations.

1908
White mobs attack Blacks in Abraham Lincoln's hometown of Springfield, Illinois.

1909
The National Association for the Advancement of Colored People (NAACP) is formed to combat racial discrimination and the suppression of African American citizenship rights.

1913

President Wilson restores racial segregation in the federal government's offices, restrooms, and cafeterias.

1917

As many as 250 Blacks are killed in the East St. Louis Massacre.

1917–1918

United States enters World War I, and an estimated 350,000 Blacks serve in segregated units to defend democracy.

1918

The first Anti-Lynching Bill that would make mob murder a federal crime was rejected by Congress. It would take more than two hundred attempts and 104 years before Congress passed the Emmett Till Anti-Lynching Bill. The bill was named after the 14-year-old murdered in 1955.

1919

Sixty race riots in more than three dozen cities occur in what comes to be known as Red Summer. Many of the victims are Black veterans returning from the war in Europe.

1920

The Nineteenth Amendment is added to the U.S. Constitution, giving women the right to vote in federal elections.

1921

As many as 300 Blacks are killed in the Tulsa [Oklahoma] Race Massacre.

1924

Indian Citizenship Act—Native Americans are granted American citizenship with the right to vote.

1939–1945

The Second World War: An estimated 1.5 million Blacks serve in segregated units of the U.S. military to fight the autocratic powers of Germany, Japan, Italy, and their Axis allies.

1944

U.S. Supreme Court upholds Executive Order 9066 to hold Japanese Americans in internment camps regardless of their American citizenship.

1948

President Harry S. Truman issues Executive Order 9981 integrating the U.S. armed forces.

1954

The U.S. Supreme Court rules in *Brown v. Board of Education of Topeka* [Kansas], overturning state laws that required separate public schools for Black and White students. The decision partially overruled the *Plessy v. Ferguson* separate-but-equal decision of 1896.

1954

Residents of Indianola, Mississippi, form the first White Citizens' Council to prevent public school integration.

1954–1975

The Vietnam War: As civil rights advocates fight for African American citizenship rights, 7,200 Black soldiers die in Vietnam fighting communism.

1955–1956

Martin Luther King Jr. successfully leads the Montgomery [Alabama] bus boycott.

1963

President John F. Kennedy sends a Civil Rights Bill to Congress. The bill would prohibit segregation in public places.

1963

Martin Luther King Jr. delivers his "I Have a Dream" speech in Washington, D.C.

1963

White terrorists bomb the Sixteenth Street Baptist Church in Birmingham, Alabama, killing four children.

1963

President John F. Kennedy is assassinated in Dallas, Texas.

1964

The Civil Rights Act proposed by President Kennedy is pushed through Congress by President Lyndon Johnson, is approved by Congress, and ends segregation in public accommodations, e.g., buses, trains, hotels, and restaurants.

1965

Malcolm X, a human rights leader who advocated that Black people use any means necessary to achieve equal rights, is assassinated in New York City.

1965

Bloody Sunday: John Lewis leads a voting rights march from Selma, Alabama, toward Montgomery. The march is brutally beaten back by Alabama state police. Lewis suffers a fractured skull.

1965

The Voting Rights Act authorizes the federal government to protect all citizens' right to vote, regardless of race. It corrected state and federal governments' failure to enforce the Fifteenth Amendment and increased the number of registered Black voters.

1968

Martin Luther King Jr. is assassinated in Memphis, Tennessee.

1986

John Lewis is elected to U.S. House of Representatives from Alabama. Lewis led the 1965 Bloody Sunday march and was beaten by Alabama state troopers.

2008

Barack Obama elected the forty-fourth President of the United States.

HISTORY CLIPS

"A Change Is Gonna Come" (official lyric video), Sam Cooke@YouTube.

"Mapping the history of racial terror," Danny Lewis (smithsonianmag. com).

"I Have a Dream," Martin Luther King Jr. full speech with subtitles @ youtube.com.

"Read the letter the FBI sent MLK to try to convince him to kill himself," @vox.com.

President Lyndon B. Johnson, "Voting Rights Address," @C-SPAN.org.

CNN Raw Video: Barack Obama 2008 acceptance speech: @youtube.com.

FURTHER READING

ENSLAVEMENT AND EMANCIPATION

Never Caught: The Story of Ona Judge (Young Readers Edition) by Erica Armstrong Dunbar and Kathleen Van Cleve. New York: Aladdin Books, 2020.

The 1619 Project: Born on the Water by Nikole Hannah-Jones and Renée Watson, illustrated by Nikkolas Smith. New York: Random House, 2021.

FREEDOM AND JUSTICE

Birmingham Sunday by Larry Dane Brimner. New York: Calkins Creek, 2010.

Finish the Fight!: The Brave and Revolutionary Women Who Fought for the Right to Vote by Veronica Chambers and the Staff of the *New York Times*. New York: Versify, 2020.

March (Books 1–3) by John Lewis, Andrew Aydin, and Nate Powell. Marietta, GA: Top Shelf Productions, 2016.

THE PROMISE OF AMERICA

Dreams from My Father: A Story of Race and Inheritance (Adapted for Young Adults) by Barack Obama. New York: Delacorte Press, 2021.

Fault Lines in the Constitution: The Graphic Novel by Cynthia Levinson and Sanford Levinson, art by Ally Shwed. New York: First Second, 2020.

Stamped: Racism, Antiracism, and You, by Jason Reynolds and Ibram X. Kendi. New York: Little, Brown Books for Young Readers, 2020.

ACKNOWLEDGMENTS

I am grateful for the support and encouragement of my family, friends, colleagues, and neighbors who periodically asked, "How's the writing going?" I am indebted to Mimsy Beckwith, Mary Chitty, David Cottingham, Sarah Jensen, Kathy Shepard, Edda Valborg Sigurðardóttir, Padma Venkatraman, and Frankie Wright. A special thanks to Kate Clifford Larson, who graciously shared her knowledge of Harriet Tubman; Carolyn P. Yoder, Calkins Creek Books' editorial director, for her confidence in this book (which was indeed a long time in the writing); and to Caryn Wiseman for her wise and timely counsel. And finally, to my fellow writers of the Boston Biography Group, thank you, and may we all keep telling our stories.

BIBLIOGRAPHY AND SOURCE NOTES

EPIGRAPH

Baldwin, James. *Nobody Knows My Name*. New York: Vintage
International, 1993, pp. 61–62.

THE WOMAN WHO STOLE HERSELF— ONA JUDGE

BIBLIOGRAPHY
Primary Sources

Adams, Rev. T. H. "Washington's Runaway Slave, and How Portsmouth
Freed Her." Concord, New Hampshire: *The Granite Freeman*, May 22,
1845.

Chase, Rev. Benjamin. *The Liberator*. Boston: January 1, 1847.

Claypoole's American Daily Advertiser. Philadelphia: May 26, 1796, p. 3.

Washington, George. *Washington Papers, Letter to Oliver Wolcott Jr.*
September 1 and November 28, 1796. Charlottesville: The Founders
Online—University of Virginia.

Whipple, Joseph. *Letter to Oliver Wolcott Jr., October 4, 1796*. George
Washington Papers, Series 4, Library of Congress.

Secondary Sources

Chernow, Ron. *Washington: A Life*. New York: Penguin, 2010.

Wieneck, Henry. *An Imperfect God: George Washington, His Slaves, and
the Creation of America*. New York: Farrar, Straus & Giroux, 2003.

Source Notes

"I am free now . . .": Adams. *The Granite Freeman*.

"nearly white . . .": Chase, p. 1.

"slender . . .": *Claypoole's American Daily Advertiser*.

"bushy black hair . . .": same as above.

"Rogue & Runaway . . .": Wieneck, p. 132.

"a Mistress of her needle . . .": Washington to Wolcott (September 1, 1796).

"Nine teeth from . . .": Chernow, p. 438.

"Blacks are so . . .": Wieneck, p. 324.

"ten dollars will be paid . . .": *Claypoole*.

"Oney! Where in . . .": Wieneck, p. 323.

"Run away . . .": same as above.

"And from such . . .": same as above.

"Yes I know . . .": same as above.

"such a trifling . . .": Washington to Wolcott (September 1, 1796).

"To seize and . . .": same as above.

"she should rather . . .": Whipple to Washington (October 4, 1796).

"reward unfaithfulness . . .": Washington to Wolcott (November 28, 1796).

"I am free now . . .": Adams.

"She'd rather suffer . . .": Whipple.

"No, I am free . . .": Adams.

THE DAY AND NIGHT WARRIORS— FREDERICK DOUGLASS AND HARRIET TUBMAN

BIBLIOGRAPHY

Primary Sources

Douglass, Frederick. *Douglass: Autobiographies*. New York: Library of America, 1994.

———. *The Frederick Douglass Papers*. Series 1, Vols. 1–5, edited by John W. Blassingame. New Haven: Yale University Press, 1979–92.

Foner, Philip S., and Yuval Taylor, eds., *Frederick Douglass: Selected Speeches and Writings*. New York: Lawrence Hill Books, 1999.

Hall, Kermit L. *The Oxford Companion to the Supreme Court of the United States*. New York: Oxford University Press, 1992.

Tubman, Harriet. *Scenes in the Life of Harriet Tubman*, edited by Sarah Bradford. Auburn, NY: W. J. Moses, 1869.

———. *Harriet Tubman: The Moses of Her People*. Mineola, NY: Dover, 1886, reprint, 2004.

Secondary Sources

Blight, David W. *Frederick Douglass: Prophet of Freedom*. New York: Simon & Schuster, 2018.

Larson, Kate Clifford. *Harriet Tubman, Portrait of an American Hero: Bound for the Promised Land*. New York: One World, 2003.

Source Notes

"The wretchedness of . . .": Douglass, *Autobiographies*, p. 89.

"There was one . . .": Tubman, *Moses*, p. 17.

"like so many . . .": Douglass, *Autobiographies*, p. 33.

"a blood-clotted . . .": Douglass, *Autobiographies*, p. 18.

"d. . .d, LASH . . .": same as above., p. 19.

"Why should such . . .": Tubman, *Moses*, p. 10.

"Why are some . . .": Douglass, *Autobiographies*, p. 178.

"pathway from slavery . . .": Douglass, *Autobiographies*, p. 38.

"vocabulary of liberation . . .": Blight, p. 44.

"mind and heart by . . .": Douglass, *Autobiographies*, p. 299.

"was esteemed to . . .": same as above.

"himself down near . . .": The Frederick Douglass Papers, p. 208.

"I was yet . . .": same as above.

"hopeless grief . . .": Tubman, *Moses*, p. 10.

"I had a right . . .": same as above, p. 17.

"Lord, if you . . .": same as above, p. 14.

"liberty or death . . .": same as above, p. 17.

"There was no . . .": same as above, p. 18.

"toil-worn and . . .": Douglass, *Autobiographies*, p. 90.

"salt water mobocrats . . .": same as above, p. 371.

"collect sufficient money . . .": same as above, p. 710.

"I never ran . . .": Larson, p. 276.

"Fellow Citizens . . .": Foner and Taylor, p. 192.

"Whether we turn . . .": the same as above, p. 195.

"were not intended . . .": Hall, p. 797.

"Drag him to . . .": Tubman, *Moses*, p. 64.

"God won't let . . .": Larson, p. 206.

"Men in earnest . . .": *Douglass' Monthly*, September 1861.

"I'd go to . . .": Tubman, *Moses*, p. 51.

"And then we . . .": Larson, p. 220.

"early every morning . . .": Tubman, *Moses*, p. 51.
"We can get . . .": Foner and Taylor, p. 527.
"Most that I . . .": Tubman, *Scenes*, p. 7.

THE REASON WHY—IDA B. WELLS

BIBLIOGRAPHY

Primary Sources

Wells, Ida B. *Crusade for Justice: The Autobiography of Ida B. Wells*, edited by Alfreda M. Duster. Chicago: University of Chicago Press, 1970.

———. *The Light of Truth: Writings of an Anti-Lynching Crusader*, edited by Mia Bay. New York: Penguin, 2014.

———. *The Reason Why the Colored American Is Not in the World's Columbian Exposition*. Manuscript/Mixed Material. loc.gov/item/mfd.25023/.

Wells-Barnett, Ida. B. *The East St. Louis Massacre: The Greatest Outrage of the Century*, 1917. digital.lib.niu.edu/islandora/object/niu-gildedage%3A24051.

———. *Selected Works of Ida B. Wells-Barnett*, edited by Trudier Harris. New York: Oxford University Press, 1991.

Wilson, Woodrow. *A History of the American People, Vol. V*. New York: Harper & Brothers, 1902.

Secondary Sources

Giddings, Paula J. *Ida: A Sword Among Lions*. New York: Amistad, 2008.

Senechal, Roberta. *In Lincoln's Shadow: The 1908 Springfield Race Riot*. Carbondale, IL: Southern Illinois University Press, 1990.

The Journal of Negro History, Vol. 5, Number 3, July 1966.

Source Notes

"The way to. . .": Wells, *The Light of Truth*, p. XIX.
"What It Costs . . .": *Memphis Daily Appeal*, December 25, 1884.
"the law of nature . . .": Giddings, p. 71.
"humane and sympathetic . . .": Wells, *Crusade*, p. 14.
"I am quite . . .": Giddings, p. 38.
"What kind of . . .": Giddings, p. 98.

"plain, common-sense . . .": Wells, *Crusade*, p. 24.

"A woman editor . . .": same as above, p. 39.

"Princess of the Press . . .": same as above, p. 33.

"Tell my people . . .": same as above, p. 51.

"one of the most . . .": Giddings, p. 183.

"The South resented . . .": Wells, *The Light of Truth*, p. 69.

"Eight Negroes lynched . . .": same as above, p. 60.

"If Southern white men . . .": same as above, p. 60.

"tied the wretch . . .": same as above, p. 61.

"'Free Speech' was . . .": same as above, p. 61.

"Since my business . . .": same as above, p. 61.

"Somebody must show . . .": same as above, p. 58.

"Brave Woman!" . . .": same as above, p. 59.

"The Nemesis of Southern . . .": Wells, *Crusade*, p. 127.

"would have been . . .": Wells, *The Light of Truth*, p. 127.

"while still married . . .": Giddings, p. 358.

"was my first . . .": Wells, *Crusade*, p. 242.

"lived for years . . .": Giddings, p. 348.

"he libeled not . . .": same as above.

"Our country's national . . .": Wells, *The Light of Truth*, p. 394.

"by the inhuman butchery . . .": same as above, p. 395.

"Lincoln freed you . . .": Senechal, p. 22.

"at the hands . . .": Giddings, p. 481.

"if we only had men . . .": same as above, p. 487.

"fair means or . . .": Wilson, p. 58.

"considered by the black . . .": Giddings, p. 599.

"Red Summer . . .": *The Journal of Negro History*, p. 341.

"nor shall any . . .": Fourteenth Amendment of the U.S. Constitution.

"ought to wipe . . .": Giddings, p. 624.

THIS LIE WILL NOT LIVE—MARTIN LUTHER KING JR.

Bibliography
Primary Sources
Dorsey, Thomas, Rev. "Take My Hand, Precious Lord." 1932.

FBI intelligence file, August 30, 1963.

Holy Bible, King James Version.

Johnson, Lyndon B. "Voting Rights Address," March 15, 1965.

King, Martin Luther Jr. *A Testament of Hope: The Essential Writings and Speeches of Martin Luther King Jr.,* edited by James Melvin Washington. New York: HarperOne, 1991.

Kennedy, John F. "Civil Rights Address," June 11, 1963.

FBI letter to Martin Luther King Jr., August 30, 1963. National Archives

Tindley, Charles Albert. "We Shall Overcome," 1901.

X, Malcolm. "Message to the Grassroots," December 10, 1963.

Secondary Sources

AP News Archives, January 7, 1994.

Branch, Taylor. *Parting the Waters: America in the King Years 1954–63.* New York: Simon and Schuster, 1988.

Decatur [AL] *Daily,* April 14, 1963.

Frady, Marshall. *Martin Luther King, Jr.* New York: Penguin, 2002.

Gentry, Curt. *J. Edgar Hoover: The Man and the Secrets.* New York: W. W. Norton, 1991.

Pratt, Robert A. *Selma's Bloody Sunday.* Baltimore: Johns Hopkins University Press, 2017.

Source Notes

"How Long . . .": King, ed. Washington, p. 230.

"love your enemies . . .": Luke 6:27, KJV.

"If I should die . . .": a common children's prayer.

"the Wreckers . . .": Frady, p. 17.

"this nigger man . . .": testimony of Carolyn Bryant.

"unwise and untimely . . .": *Decatur Daily.*

"disperse 'or you're . . .'": Branch, p. 758.

"We are confronted . . .": President John F. Kennedy.

"of color . . .": same as above.

"You just wait until after Sunday . . .": *AP News Archives.*

"the most dangerous . . .": FBI intelligence file.

"You are a colossal . . .": FBI letter to Martin Luther King Jr.

"You don't have . . .": Malcolm X.

"largely because of their . . .": Pratt, p. 36.

"You see, most . . .": same as above, pp. 36–37.

"This march will . . .": same as above, p. 73.

"It is not just . . .": President Lyndon B. Johnson.

"I knew that . . .": King, ed., Washington, ed., p. 233.

"What is that . . .": theintercept.com.

"Rabble-Rouser Index . . .": Gentry, p. 602.

"mine eyes have . . .": "The Battle Hymn of the Republic."

"But I say unto you . . .": Luke 6:27, KJV.

"Precious Lord": Rev. Dorsey.

"Let us die . . .": "The Battle Hymn of the Republic."

"We Shall Overcome": Tindley.

"We shall live . . .": same as above.

PERSONAL HISTORY

"Besides, They'll see . . .": Hughes, Langston. "I Too." p. 46. Rampersad, Arnold, ed. *The Collected Poems of Langston Hughes*. New York: Knopf, 1994.

THE AUDACITY OF RACE— BARACK OBAMA

BIBLIOGRAPHY
Primary Sources
Obama, Barack. *Dreams from My Father*. New York: Three Rivers Press, 1995.

———. *Dreams from My Father*, YA Edition New York, Delacorte Press, 2021.

———. *A Promised Land*. New York: Crown, 2020.

———. "A More Perfect Union." Transcripts Wire. March 18, 2008.

———. "This Is Your Victory." Transcript Wire. Chicago: November 4, 2008.

Obama, Michelle. *Becoming*. New York: Crown, 2018.

Smith, Samuel Francis. Lyrics "My Country 'Tis of Thee," 1831.

Secondary Sources

Garrow, David J. *Rising Star: The Making of Barack Obama*. New York: William Morrow, 2017.

Senechal, Roberta. *In Lincoln's Shadow: The 1908 Springfield Race Riot*. Carbondale, IL: Southern Illinois University Press, 1990.

Source Notes

"My identity might . . .": Obama, *Dreams from My Father*, p. 111.

"Coffee with cream . . .": Garrow, p. 52.

"should be one . . .": Obama, *Dreams from My Father*, p. 63.

"raise myself to be . . .": same as above (YA Edition), p. 68.

"I shouldn't touch . . .": same as above, p. 77.

"good-time Charlie . . .": same as above, p. 91.

"Look at Gramps . . .": same as above, p. 91 (YA edition).

"Do we settle . . .": Obama, Michelle. *Becoming*, p. 118.

"I could somehow . . .": Obama, *Dreams from My Father*, p. 347.

"This voice of authority . . .": Garrow, p. 340.

"Lincoln freed you . . .": Senechal, p. 22.

"stained by this . . .": Obama, "A More Perfect Union."

"to narrow the gap . . .": same as above.

"It's been a . . .": Obama, "This Is Your Victory."

"I will never . . .": Obama, "A More Perfect Union."

"Sweet land of . . .": Smith.

INDEX

A

Abernathy, Ralph, 195, 198, 203
abolitionists
    anti-slavery activism of Douglass,
        77, 78, 82, 83; of Tubman, 86,
        89–91, 96, 104–105, 108, 115; of
        William Lloyd Garrison, 77–78, 79
African Methodist Episcopal Church
    (AME), 24, 58, 76
Amendments to the Constitution
    Thirteenth (abolished slavery)
        (1865), 114, 126, 127, 305, 306;
        Fourteenth (citizenship for former
        slaves) (1868), 114, 127, 171, 307;
        Fifteenth (right to vote for Black
        men) (1870), 115, 127, 227, 307, 312;
        Nineteenth (right to vote for
        women) (1920), 170, 227, 309
anti-lynching bills, U.S. Congress,
    172–173, 309
anti-lynching crusade of Ida B.
    Wells, 145–146, 149–150,
    152–155, 157, 159, 161, 167

B

Birmingham, Alabama (1963)
    bombings in, 207, 208, 215, 311;
    and "Bull" Connor, 201, 202,
    205–207, 209, 214, 244; children
    protesters in, 204–207, 210;
    deaths of children and teens in,
    215; as Magic City vs. Tragic
    City, 200–202; MLK arrested in,
    203–204; and Sixteenth Street
    Baptist Church, 205–206, 214,
    311
"birtherism" lie, 289–290

Black freedom fighters (1790s), 30
Black newspapers, 83, 133–137, 149
Black soldiers
    in American Revolution, 303;
        Civil War, 103, 105–106,
        107–112; WWI, 162, 309;
        WWII, 310; Vietnam War, 311
Bloody Sunday (Selma, Alabama,
    1965), 221–223, 227, 312
Brown, John, 93–96, 100, 305

C

Cairo, Illinois, lynchings (1909),
    158–159
Chicago, Illinois
    Columbian Exposition (1893),
        147–148; first Black mayor of
        (1983), 273; and Ida B. Wells,
        146–149, 159, 164–167, 170,
        173–174, 209; MLK and family
        in, 231–232; Obama in, 273–276,
        278, 282, 284, 290, 293, 295;
        public housing, 231, 274–276;
        segregation in, 231–232;
        17-day riot (1919), after murder
        of Eugene Williams, 165–167;
        South Side of, 273, 283
Civil Rights Act (1964), 209–213,
    216–217, 219, 233, 244, 287,
    307, 311
civil rights movement, 194, 213, 250,
    266, 287, 307
Civil War, 99, 100, 112, 114, 122–
    123, 162, 178–179, 249, 305–306
    Black soldiers in, 103, 105, 106,
        108, 110–112; and Confederacy,
        105; and Douglass, 103, 106,
        109–112; and myth of race, 113–
        115; post-war White rage, 145,

208; secession (1861), 102, 305; slave refugees during, 104–105, 122; Tubman's work in, 104–110

color codes, 179–180, 188, 198, 200–201, 202, 212–213, 219, 229, 273, 274

color line, 19, 82, 142, 143, 165

Constitution, U.S., 23, 45, 102, 105, 126, 212, 213, 289, 292, 303–304, 307, 309. *See also* Amendments.

D

Declaration of Independence, 23, 45, 91, 213, 303

Douglass, Frederick, 42–113, 115-117 activism, as Black warrior, 77, 78; and Anna Murray (wife), 58–60, 74–76, 82; apprenticeship as ship caulker, 57–58; autobiography (1845), 79–80; childhood, enslaved, 46, 48–49; children of, 76, 95, 106, 109–110; and Civil War, 103, 105, 106, 110–113; death (1895), 116; escape from slavery (1838), 59–61, 74, 299; freedom purchased, 82; as fugitive outlaw (1838–1847), 60, 73, 74, 76, 80–82, 95, 305; and John Brown, 94–95, 305; and Lincoln, 112; literacy and, 53, 54–55, 79–80; mob attacks on, 79, 81–82; mother, Harriet Bailey, 46, 49; in New Bedford, Massachusetts, 74–76; *North Star* newspaper founded by (1847), 83; and Underground Railroad, 83

Dred Scott decision (1857), 92, 93, 305

E

East St. Louis, Illinois, massacre (1917), 162–164, 309

Ebenezer Baptist Church, Atlanta, 200, 232

Edmund Pettus Bridge (Selma, 1965), 223, 225

Emancipation Proclamation (1863), 105, 106, 296, 306

F

54th Massachusetts Infantry, 106, 109–110, 112

fugitive outlaws. *See under* Judge, Ona; Douglass, Frederick; Tubman, Harriet

Fugitive Slave Acts (1793), 26, 304–305, and (1850) "Bloodhound Law," 85, 89, 91, 96, 305

G

Gandhi, Mohandas, 189, 196, 219

gender discrimination, 115, 131, 164

Guardians of the Lie, 179–181, 183, 186, 188, 194, 198, 199, 204, 207, 213–215, 228–230, 233–234, 244, 245, 248, 250, 300–301

H

Hoover, J. Edgar, 166, 209, 218-219, 236, 241

I

I AM A MAN worker strike and riot, Memphis (1968), 238–239

"I Have a Dream" speech (1963), 212–213

J

Jim Crow and segregation, 126, 187–188, 192, 207, 307 NAACP formed to fight, 156–157; as slavery's next of kin, 126, 151, 189; violence and, 137, 141, 150–151, 153, 158, 199, 208, 250; Wells's activism against, 141–142, 149, 150–151, 153–154, 158–159, 161, 174, 296

Johnson, Lyndon B., 218, 227, 233, 234, 247, 311

Jubilee Day and the Emancipation Proclamation (1863), 106, 296

Judge, Ona, 11–41
and Betty (mother), 16, 17, 18, 19, 20, 27–28; capture attempts by Washingtons, 32, 33–34, 37–40; childhood at Mount Vernon, 15–17; children of, 36, 38, 39, 40; death of (1848), 40-41; and Eliza Washington Law, 24–25, 29, 34; escape of (1796), 31, 299; father Andrew Judge, 19; as First Maid (1789), 22, 28; and freedom, thoughts of, 25, 30–32, 39, 41; husband Jack Staines, 36; from runaway to fugitive outlaw, 26: remaining years as fugitive outlaw, 31–41; Separation Day of, 16, 17, 28; siblings of, 18, 19, 22, 27, 34

K

Kennedy, John, F., 209–211, 216, 311

King, Coretta Scott, 190–193, 197, 203, 216, 218, 228, 231, 241, 247

King, Martin Luther Jr., Dr., 176–251, anti-poverty efforts, 235–236, 241, 247; assassination (1968), 239–249; in Atlanta, 178, 183, 184, 200, 223, 224, 232, 239; and attacks on Birmingham protesters, 206–208; Bloody Sunday and death of Jimmie Lee Jackson, 222; in Chicago, 231–232; children of, 193, 231; civil rights movement, as voice of, 212-213, 250; and Daddy King (father), 180, 183, 190, 191, 200, 223, 247; Gandhi, Mohandas, influence of, 189, 196, 219; Hoover, J. Edgar and FBI actions against, 209, 210, 218–219, 234, 235, 236, 237, 241; "I Have a Dream" speech (1963), 212–213, 292, 311; Johnson, Lyndon B. and, 227, 233; "Letter from Birmingham City Jail" (1963), 203–204; and Liuzzo, Viola Gregg, shooting of, 229; Man of the Year, *Time* (1964), 217; March on Washington (1963), 212–213, 236; "most dangerous Negro," 218, 237, 250; "Mountaintop" sermon, Mason Temple, Memphis (1968), 243–246; "The Negro and the Constitution" oration, age 185, 211-212; Nobel Peace Prize award (1964), 217; nonviolent protests and, 189, 202, 214, 217, 219; as protest preacher, 181, 198, 216, 228, 233, 243, 247, 300; statue on National Mall, 250; and teenage crusaders in protests, 204–205; on Vietnam

War, 233, 235, 239, 247. *See also* Abernathy, Ralph; King, Coretta Scott; Lewis, John.

L

Lewis, John, 223, 225, 312

Liberty, running for, 21, 24, 29, 30–31, 59–60, 62–63, 68–69, 73, 74, 85

Liberty Bell, 23, 26, 299

Lincoln, Abraham, 102, 103, 111, 112, 113, 155, 156, 172, 287, 299, 306

Lincoln Memorial, 212

lynchings. *See* anti-lynching crusade of Ida B. Wells and pamphlets of Ida B. Wells.

M

Malcolm X, 220, 221, 312

Mandela, Nelson, 270

Martin Luther King Day (MLK Day), 251

Memphis, Tennessee assassination of MLK (1968), 248, 312; Black sanitation workers' strike (1968), 237–238; the Curve, and lynching of Tommie Moss and two friends (1892), 137–140, 142; FBI informants in, 240; "I've Been to the Mountaintop," MLK sermon (1968), 243–246; *Memphis Free Speech and Headlight* newspaper, 134; Wells, teaching and journalism in, 133–144 and exile from (1892), 145

Montgomery, Alabama bombings in, 198–199; bus boycott (strike), 195–198, 200, 209, 311; First Baptist, Black church in, 195; King preaching in, 193

Mount Vernon, Virginia, 15–21, 27, 28, 29, 36–39

mulatto, negative meaning of, 18, 125

N

Narrative of the Life of Frederick Douglass, The, 79–80

National Association for the Advancement of Colored People (NAACP) (1909), 156–157, 308

North Star, the, celestial guide for fugitives, 61, 69, 300

North Star, newspaper, founded by Frederick Douglass, 83

O

Obama, Barack, 254–297 "A More Perfect Union" speech on race (2008), 292; "birtherism" lie about, 289–290; community organizing, 272–276, 278, 286, 290; daughters (Malia and Sasha), 284, 291; decision to run for President, 286–288; education, 258, 260, 266–268, 269–270, 282–284; election to Presidency (2008), 293–295, 296–297; father, Barack Obama Sr., 257, 261–265, 271, 276–277, 281; grandparents, 261, 263, 265, 267, 280; half-sister Auma, 276, 277, 279; half-sister Maya, 260, 265, 266, 285; *Harvard Law Review,* president of, 283; Harvard Law School, 282; mother, Stanley Ann

Dunham, 257, 258, 260, 261, 262, 263, 265, 266, 268, 277, 285; race, questions and consequences, 259, 266–267, 269–270, 274–276, 288–289, 292–293; relatives in in Kenya, 279–281; Reverend Wright and, 290–291, 293; as state senator, Illinois, 285; stepfather, Lolo Soetoro, 258; as U.S. Senator, Illinois (2004), 286; and Yes, We Can, 286

Obama, Michelle (Robinson), 283–286, 291

P

pamphlets of Ida B. Wells (list of, from 1892 to 1900), 145, 146, 149, 154, 164, 169–170

Parks, Rosa, 194–197

"persons unknown," murderers of those lynched, 172–173

Philadelphia, Pennsylvania, 23, 25–28, 30, 32–35, 45, 60, 69, 95, 143

Poor People's Campaign, of MLK (1967), 235–236, 237, 241

R

Red Record, The, 149–151, 154

Red Summer (1919), James Weldon Johnson, 168, 309

S

segregation, racial, 189, 192, 200, 207, 216, 231, 235, 250, 308–309, 311. *See also* Jim Crow.

Selma to Montgomery march (1965), 221–230, 312

South Carolina, secession of, 102–103

Southern Christian Leadership Conference (SCLC), 200

Springfield, Illinois

Lincoln and, 102; race riots and lynching (1908), 155–156, 308, and Wells investigation of, 159

Supreme Court, U.S.

frees Arkansas death row Blacks (1927), 173–174; overturns state laws requiring separate schools for Black and White students (1954), 310; rules against Black citizenship (1857), 92–93, 305; rules against Montgomery bus segregation (1956), 198, 243; upholds segregation (1896), 308

T

Till, Emmett, murder of (1955), 118, 194, 195, 309

Tubman, Harriet (Araminta "Minty" Ross), 43–117

activism, 89, 96, 115, 151–152; childhood, enslaved, 50–52, 116–117; in Civil War as Union nurse, scout, and spy, 104–105, 106, 110; death (1913), 116; enslaved family broken up, 47, 50, 63; escape from slavery, 66–67, 68–69, 72–73; father, Ben Ross, who taught her how to find the North Star, 61; as fugitive outlaw, 69, 73, 89–91; head injury (age 14) and aftereffects, 61–63; husband John Tubman, 64, 66–67, 68, 84, 88–90; memoirs of (1869), 115; in Military Intelligence Corps Hall of Fame, 296; missions north, leading others to freedom, 70, 86–91, 99–100; as Moses, Biblical story taught to, by mother Rit, 61, 90–91, 106; and Underground Railroad, 90–91, 152

U

Underground Railroad, 68, 74, 83, 91, 152

V

Voting rights (suffrage), 115, 127, 160, 170, 221, 222, 224, 227, 228, 235, 245, 306, 307, 309, 310
Voting Rights Act (1965), 227, 233, 245, 287, 288, 312

W

Washington, George, 15, 17–22, 24, 26–27, 33–35, 85, 292, 303
Washington, Martha (Custis), 15–17, 18, 19, 22, 25, 29, 32, 35, 36–37
Wells, Ida B. (Wells-Barnett), 120–175
  anti-lynching newspaper reporting of, 141–142, 145–146, 149–151; birth (1862), 127; C&O Railroad lawsuit (1884), 123–125; care of five siblings (at age 16) after parents' deaths, 129–133; champion for Black achievement since slavery, 147–148; denied passport (1919), 167; endorsed by Douglass, 151; investigative reporting on Tommie Moss lynching (1892) and reaction to, 137–145; J. Edgar Hoover lists Wells as "troublemaker," 166; lifelong lessons from parents, 129; marriage to Ferdinand Barnett (1895), 149; and NAACP, 156–157; newspaper publishing, 134–137, 144–145; pamphlet publishing exposing Jim Crow racial terror and legal injustices, 154, 158–159, 162–164, 168–170, 308; as teacher (at age 16), in Holly Springs, MS, 132, and in Memphis, 135; Tennessee Supreme Court ruling about Ida's ancestry, 125; in Washington, D.C., 151–153, 160–161
White superiority, belief in, 78, 125, 126, 179, 180, 248, 250
  See also Guardians of the Lie; Jim Crow and segregation.
Wilson, Woodrow, support of racial segregation, 161, 309
women's suffrage
  march (1913) and Ida B. Wells, 160; Nineteenth Amendment and, 227, 309

ABOUT THE AUTHOR

In many ways, this book is my personal history, a chronicle of the times of my grandparents, parents, and me—149 years of hands upon hands stretching through the decades of the Long Time. My mother's father (1859–1939) was an enslaved child until he was emancipated in 1865. My grandparents lived during the times of Frederick Douglass, Harriet Tubman, and Ida B. Wells. My mother (1919–2004), a daughter of a slave, and my father (1915–2007), a great-grandson of a slave, lived through the betrayal times of race-restricted jobs, housing, and "colored" public schools in the era of Ida B. Wells and Martin Luther King Jr.

I was born a decade before the civil rights movement and felt the bite of racial hatred and ignorance, but not with the same viciousness or disappointments as my parents or grandparents. I stumbled through the racial fog, guided by the promise of the American dream as I zigzagged through its nightmarish traumas. I vividly recall the assassinations of John F. Kennedy, Malcolm X (whom I heard speak), and Martin Luther King Jr. as well as the murders of Emmett Till and many civil rights soldiers. I marched in demonstrations in the North, attended graduate school on a Martin Luther King Jr. fellowship, and my wife and I marched in a 2007 New Hampshire Labor Day Parade with Barack Obama.

In short, I have lived and touched the hands of others who have lived in the stories I chronicle here. Now I'm the grandfather in the room, and this book is my gift to my children's children and their generation. I am blessed to be able to share it.

Visit rayanthonyshepard.com

TEXT CREDITS

For information about permission to reproduce selections from this book, please contact permissions@astrapublishinghouse.com.

Calkins Creek
An imprint of Astra Books for Young Readers,
a division of Astra Publishing House
astrapublishinghouse.com
Printed in China

ISBN: 978-1-6626-8066-3 (hc)
ISBN: 978-1-6626-8067-0 (eBook)

Publisher's Cataloging-in-Publication data

Names: Shepherd, Ray Anthony, author. | Christie, R. Gregory, illustrator.
Title: A long time coming : a lyrical biography of race in America from Ona Judge to Barack Obama / Ray Anthony Shepard; art by R. Gregory Christie.
Description: Includes bibliographical references and index. | New York, NY: Calkins Creek, an Imprint of Astra Books for Young Readers, 2023.
Identifiers: LCCN: 2020947716 | ISBN: 9781662680663 (hardcover) | 9781662680670 (ebook)
Subjects: LCSH African Americans--Biography--Juvenile literature. | African Americans--History--Juvenile literature. | Poetry, American. | BISAC JUVENILE NONFICTION / Biography & Autobiography / Historical | JUVENILE NONFICTION / Biography & Autobiography / Cultural, Ethnic & Regional | POETRY / American / General | POETRY / American / African American and Black. | JUVENILE NONFICTION / Poetry / General
Classification: LCC E185.96 .S44 2023 | DDC 920.0092/96073--dc23

First edition

10 9 8 7 6 5 4 3 2 1

Design by Barbara Grzeslo
The text is set in Sabon LT Std.
The titles are set in Rockwell Std and Bourton.
The art is done in Acryla gouache on
illustration board and India ink on paper.

333